A SHORT HISTORY
OF MYTH

Also by Karen Armstrong

The Spiral Staircase: My Climb Out of Darkness (2004)

Buddha (2001)

Islam: A Short History (2000)

The Battle for God (2000)

Jerusalem: One City, Three Faiths (1996)

In the Beginning: A New Interpretation of Genesis (1996)

Visions of God: Four Medieval Mystics and Their Writings (1994)

*A History of God: The 4000-Year Quest of Judaism,
Christianity and Islam* (1993)

Muhammad: A Biography of the Prophet (1992)

The English Mystics of the Fourteenth Century (ed.) (1991)

*Holy War: The Crusades and Their
Impact on Today's World* (1998)

*The Gospel According to Woman: Christianity's Creation of
the Sex War in the West* (1986)

*Tongues of Fire: An Anthology of Religious and Poetic
Experience* (ed.) (1985)

The First Christian: St. Paul's Impact on Christianity (1983)

Beginning the World (1983)

*Through the Narrow Gate: A Memoir of Life In and Out
of the Convent* (1981)

Myths are universal and timeless stories that reflect and shape our lives — they mirror our desires, our fears, our longings, and provide narratives that attempt to help us make sense of the world. The Myths series brings together some of the finest writers of our time to provide a contemporary take on our most enduring stories. Authors in the series also include Chinua Achebe, Margaret Atwood, A.S. Byatt, David Grossman, Milton Hatoum, Victor Pelevin, Donna Tartt, Su Tong and Jeanette Winterson.

A SHORT HISTORY
OF MYTH

Karen Armstrong

Alfred A. Knopf Canada

PUBLISHED BY ALFRED A. KNOPF CANADA

Copyright © 2005 Karen Armstrong
Published by agreement with Canongate Books Ltd., Edinburgh, Scotland

www.randomhouse.ca

Library and Archives Canada Cataloguing in Publication

Armstrong, Karen, 1944–
    A short history of myth / Karen Armstrong.

(The myths series)
Includes bibliographical references.
ISBN 0-676-97419-8

1. Myth—History. 2. Mythology—History. I. Title. II. Series: Myths
series.

BL304.A76 2005   398.2   C2005-901014-2

Series, cover and logo design © Pentagram
Illustration by Roderick Mills
Calligraphy by Peter Horridge
Typeset in Van Dijck by Palimpsest Book Production Ltd, Polmont,
Stirlingshire

First Edition

Printed and bound in Canada

This book is printed on ancient-forest friendly, 100% recycled, 100% post-
consumer waste paper.

10 9 8 7 6 5 4 3 2 1

CONTENTS

What is a Myth?

Human beings have always been mythmakers. Archaeologists have unearthed Neanderthal graves containing weapons, tools and the bones of a sacrificed animal, all of which suggest some kind of belief in a future world that was similar to their own. The Neanderthals may have told each other stories about the life that their dead companion now enjoyed. They were certainly reflecting about death in a way that their fellow-creatures did not. Animals watch each other die but, as far as we know, they give the matter no further consideration. But the Neanderthal graves show that when these early people became conscious of their mortality, they created some sort of counter-narrative that enabled them to come to terms with it. The Neanderthals who buried their companions with such care seem to have imagined that the visible, material world was not the only reality. From a very early date, therefore, it appears that human beings were distinguished by their ability to have ideas that went beyond their everyday experience.

We are meaning-seeking creatures. Dogs, as far as we know, do not agonise about the canine condition, worry about the plight of dogs in other parts of the world, or try to see their lives from a different perspective. But human beings fall easily into despair, and from the very beginning we invented stories that enabled us to place our lives in a larger setting, that revealed an underlying pattern, and gave us a sense that, against all the depressing and chaotic evidence to the contrary, life had meaning and value.

Another peculiar characteristic of the human mind is its ability to have ideas and experiences that we cannot explain rationally. We have imagination, a faculty that enables us to think of something that is not immediately present, and that, when we first conceive it, has no objective existence. The imagination is the faculty that produces religion and mythology. Today mythical thinking has fallen into disrepute; we often dismiss it as irrational and self-indulgent. But the imagination is also the faculty that has enabled scientists to bring new knowledge to light and to invent technology that has made us immeasurably more effective. The imagination of scientists has enabled us to travel through outer space and walk on the moon, feats that were once only possible in the realm of myth. Mythology and science both extend the scope of human beings. Like science and technology, mythology, as we shall see, is not about opting out of this world, but about enabling us to live more intensely within it.

The Neanderthal graves tell us five important things about myth. First, it is nearly always rooted in the experience of death and the fear of extinction. Second, the animal bones indicate that the burial was accompanied by a sacrifice. Mythology is usually inseparable from ritual. Many myths make no sense outside a liturgical drama that brings them to life, and are incomprehensible in a profane setting. Third, the Neanderthal myth was in some way recalled beside a grave, at the limit of human life. The most powerful myths are about extremity; they force us to go beyond our experience. There are moments when we all, in one way or another, have to go to a place that we have never seen, and do what we have never done before.

Myth is about the unknown; it is about that for which initially we have no words. Myth therefore looks into the heart of a great silence. Fourth, myth is not a story told for its own sake. It shows us how we should behave. In the Neanderthal graves, the corpse has sometimes been placed in a foetal position, as though for rebirth: the deceased had to take the next step himself. Correctly understood, mythology puts us in the correct spiritual or psychological posture for right action, in this world or the next.

Finally, all mythology speaks of another plane that exists alongside our own world, and that in some sense supports it. Belief in this invisible but more powerful reality, sometimes called the world of the gods, is a basic theme of mythology. It has been called the 'perennial philosophy' because it informed the mythology, ritual and social organisation of all societies before the advent of our scientific modernity, and continues to influence more traditional societies today. According to the perennial philosophy, everything that happens in this world, everything that we can hear and see here below has its counterpart in the divine realm, which is richer, stronger and more enduring than our own.[1] And every earthly reality is only a pale shadow of its archetype, the original pattern, of which it is simply an imperfect copy. It is only by participating in this divine life that mortal, fragile human beings fulfil their potential. The myths gave explicit shape and form to a reality that people sensed intuitively. They told them how the gods behaved, not out of idle curiosity or because these tales were entertaining, but to enable men and women to imitate these powerful beings and experience divinity themselves.

In our scientific culture, we often have rather simplistic notions of the divine. In the ancient world, the 'gods' were rarely regarded as supernatural beings with discrete personalities, living a totally separate metaphysical existence. Mythology was not about theology, in the modern sense, but about human experience. People thought that gods, humans, animals and nature were inextricably bound up together, subject to the same laws, and composed of the same divine substance. There was initially no ontological gulf between the world of the gods and the world of men and women. When people spoke of the divine, they were usually talking about an aspect of the mundane. The very existence of the gods was inseparable from that of a storm, a sea, a river, or from those powerful human emotions – love, rage or sexual passion – that seemed momentarily to lift men and women onto a different plane of existence so that they saw the world with new eyes.

Mythology was therefore designed to help us to cope with the problematic human predicament. It helped people to find their place in the world and their true orientation. We all want to know where we came from, but because our earliest beginnings are lost in the mists of prehistory, we have created myths about our forefathers that are not historical but help to explain current attitudes about our environment, neighbours and customs. We also want to know where we are going, so we have devised stories that speak of a posthumous existence – though, as we shall see, not many myths envisage immortality for human beings. And we want to explain those sublime moments, when we seem to be transported beyond our ordinary concerns. The gods helped to explain the experience of transcendence. The perennial philosophy expresses our innate sense that there is more to human beings and to the material world than meets the eye.

Today the word 'myth' is often used to describe something that is simply not true. A politician accused of a peccadillo will say that it is a 'myth', that it never happened. When we hear of gods walking the earth, of dead men striding out of tombs, or of seas miraculously parting to let a favoured people escape from their enemies, we dismiss these stories as incredible and demonstrably untrue. Since the eighteenth century, we have developed a scientific view of history; we are concerned above all with what actually happened. But in the pre-modern world, when people wrote about the past they were more concerned with what an event had meant. A myth was an event which, in some sense, had happened once, but which also happened all the time. Because of our strictly chronological view of history, we have no word for such an occurrence, but mythology is an art form that points beyond history to what is timeless in human existence, helping us to get beyond the chaotic flux of random events, and glimpse the core of reality.

An experience of transcendence has always been part of the human experience. We seek out moments of ecstasy, when we feel deeply touched within and lifted momentarily beyond ourselves. At such times, it seems that we are living more intensely than usual, firing on all cylinders, and inhabiting the whole of our humanity. Religion has been one of the most traditional ways of attaining ecstasy, but if people no longer find it in temples, synagogues, churches or mosques, they look for it elsewhere: in art, music, poetry, rock, dance, drugs, sex or sport. Like poetry and music, mythology should awaken us to rapture, even in the face of death and the despair we may feel at the prospect of annihilation. If a myth ceases to do that, it has died and outlived its usefulness.

It is, therefore, a mistake to regard myth as an inferior mode of thought, which can be cast aside when human beings have attained the age of reason. Mythology is not an early attempt at history, and does not claim that its tales are objective fact. Like a novel, an opera or a ballet, myth is make-believe; it is a game that transfigures our fragmented, tragic world, and helps us to glimpse new possibilities by asking 'what if?' – a question which has also provoked some of our most important discoveries in philosophy, science and technology. The Neanderthals who prepared their dead companion for a new life were, perhaps, engaged in the same game of spiritual make-believe that is common to all mythmakers: 'What if this world were not all that there is? How would this affect our lives – psychologically, practically or socially? Would we become different? More complete? And, if we did find that we were so transformed, would that not show that our mythical belief was true in some way, that it was telling us something important about our humanity, even though we could not prove this rationally?'

Human beings are unique in retaining the capacity for play.[2] Unless they are living in the artificial conditions of captivity, other animals lose their early sense of fun when they encounter the harsh realities of life in the wild. Human adults, however, continue to enjoy playing with different possibilities, and, like children, we go on creating imaginary worlds. In art, liberated from the constraints of reason and logic, we conceive and combine new forms that enrich our lives, and which we believe tell us something important and profoundly 'true'. In mythology too, we entertain a hypothesis, bring it to life by means of ritual, act upon it, contemplate its effect upon our lives, and discover that we have achieved new insight into the disturbing puzzle of our world.

A myth, therefore, is true because it is effective, not because it gives us factual information. If, however, it does not give us new insight into the deeper meaning of life, it has failed. If it *works*, that is, if it forces us to change our minds and hearts, gives us new hope, and compels us to live more fully, it is a valid myth. Mythology will only transform us if we follow its directives. A myth is essentially a guide; it tells us what we must do in order to live more richly. If we do not apply it to our own situation and make the myth a reality in our own lives, it will remain as incomprehensible and remote as the rules of a board game, which often seem confusing and boring until we start to play.

Our modern alienation from myth is unprecedented. In the pre-modern world, mythology was indispensable. It not only helped people to make sense of their lives but also revealed regions of the human mind that would otherwise have remained inaccessible. It was an early form of psychology. The stories of gods or heroes descending into the underworld, threading through labyrinths and fighting with monsters, brought to light the mysterious workings of the psyche, showing people how to cope with their own interior crises. When Freud and Jung began to chart the modern quest for the soul, they instinctively turned to classical mythology to explain their insights, and gave the old myths a new interpretation.

There was nothing new in this. There is never a single, orthodox version of a myth. As our circumstances change, we need to tell our stories differently in order to bring out their timeless truth. In this short history of mythology, we shall see that every time men and women took a major step forward, they reviewed their mythology and made it speak to the new conditions. But we shall also see that human nature does not change much, and that many of these myths, devised in societies that could not be more different from our own, still address our most essential fears and desires.

The Palaeolithic Period: The Mythology of the Hunters (*c*. 20000 to 8000 BCE)

The period in which human beings completed their biological evolution is one of the longest and most formative in their history. It was in many ways a frightening and desperate time. These early people had not yet developed agriculture. They could not grow their own food, but depended entirely on hunting and gathering. Mythology was as essential to their survival as the hunting weapons and skills that they evolved in order to kill their prey and achieve a degree of control over their environment. Like the Neanderthals, Palaeolithic men and women could leave no written record of their myths, but these stories proved to be so crucial to the way that human beings understood themselves and their predicament that they survived, in fragmented form, in the mythologies of later literate cultures. We can also

learn a great deal about the experience and preoccupations of these primal human beings from such
indigenous peoples as the Pygmies or the Australian
aborigines who, like the people of the Palaeolithic
age, live in hunting societies and have not undergone
an agricultural revolution.

It is natural for these indigenous peoples to think
in terms of myth and symbol because, ethnologists
and anthropologists tell us, they are highly conscious
of a spiritual dimension in their daily lives. The
experience of what we call the sacred or the divine
has become at best a distant reality to men and
women in industrialised, urban societies, but to the
Australians, for example, it is not only self-evident
but more real than the material world. 'Dreamtime' –
which Australians experience in sleep and in
moments of vision – is timeless and 'everywhen'. It
forms a stable backdrop to ordinary life, which is
dominated by death, flux, the endless succession of
events, and the cycle of the seasons. Dreamtime is
inhabited by the Ancestors – powerful, archetypal
beings who taught humans the skills that are essential to their lives, such as hunting, war, sex, weaving

and basket-making. These are, therefore, not profane but sacred activities, which bring mortal men and women into contact with Dreamtime. When an Australian goes hunting, for example, he models his behaviour so closely on that of the First Hunter that he feels totally at one with him, caught up in that more powerful archetypal world. It is only when he experiences this mystical unity with Dreamtime that his life has meaning. Afterwards, he falls away from that primal richness and back into the world of time, which, he fears, will devour him and reduce all that he does to nothingness.[3]

The spiritual world is such an immediate and compelling reality that, the indigenous peoples believe, it must once have been more accessible to human beings. In every culture, we find the myth of a lost paradise, in which humans lived in close and daily contact with the divine. They were immortal, and lived in harmony with one another, with animals and with nature. At the centre of the world there was a tree, a mountain, or a pole, linking earth and heaven, which people could easily climb to reach the realm of the gods. Then there was a catastrophe:

the mountain collapsed, the tree was cut down, and it became more difficult to reach heaven. The story of the Golden Age, a very early and almost universal myth, was never intended to be historical. It springs from a strong experience of the sacred that is natural to human beings, and expresses their tantalising sense of a reality that is almost tangible and only just out of reach. Most of the religions and mythologies of archaic societies are imbued with longing for the lost paradise.[4] The myth was not simply an exercise in nostalgia, however. Its primary purpose was to show people how they could return to this archetypal world, not only in moments of visionary rapture but in the regular duties of their daily lives.

Today we separate the religious from the secular. This would have been incomprehensible to the Palaeolithic hunters, for whom nothing was profane. Everything they saw or experienced was transparent to its counterpart in the divine world. Anything, however lowly, could embody the sacred.[5] Everything they did was a sacrament that put them in touch with the gods. The most ordinary actions were ceremonies that enabled mortal beings to participate in the timeless world of 'everywhen'. For us moderns, a symbol is essentially separate from the unseen reality to which it directs our attention, but the Greek *symballein* means 'to throw together': two hitherto disparate objects become inseparable – like gin and tonic in a cocktail. When you contemplated any earthly object, you were therefore in the presence of its heavenly counterpart. This sense of participation in the divine was essential to the mythical world-view: the purpose of a myth was to make people more fully conscious of the spiritual dimension that surrounded them on all sides and was a natural part of life.

The earliest mythologies taught people to see through the tangible world to a reality that seemed to embody *something else*.[6] But this required no leap of faith, because at this stage there seemed to be no metaphysical gulf between the sacred and the profane. When these early people looked at a stone, they did not see an inert, unpromising rock. It embodied strength, permanence, solidity and an absolute mode of being that was quite different from the vulnerable human state. Its very otherness made it holy. A stone was a common hierophany – revelation of the sacred – in the ancient world. Again, a tree, which had the power effortlessly to renew itself, incarnated and made visible a miraculous vitality denied to mortal men and women. When they watched the waning and waxing of the moon, people saw yet another instance of sacred powers of regeneration,[7] evidence of a law that was harsh and merciful, and frightening as well as consoling. Trees, stones and heavenly bodies were never objects of worship in themselves but were revered because they were epiphanies of a hidden force that could be seen powerfully at work in all natural phenomena, giving people intimations of another, more potent reality.

Some of the very earliest myths, probably dating back to the Palaeolithic period, were associated with the sky, which seems to have given people their first notion of the divine. When they gazed at the sky – infinite, remote and existing quite apart from their puny lives – people had a religious experience.[8] The sky towered above them, inconceivably immense, inaccessible and eternal. It was the very essence of transcendence and otherness. Human beings could do nothing to affect it. The endless drama of its thunderbolts, eclipses, storms, sunsets, rainbows and meteors spoke of another endlessly active dimension, which had a dynamic life of its own. Contemplating the sky filled people with dread and delight, with awe and fear. The sky attracted them and repelled them. It was by its very nature numinous, in the way described by the great historian of religion, Rudolf Otto. In itself, without any imaginary deity behind it, the sky was *mysterium tremendum, terribile et fascinans*.[9]

This introduces us to an essential element of both the mythical and the religious consciousness. In our sceptical age, it is often assumed that people are religious because they want something from the gods they worship. They are trying to get the Powers That Be on their side. They want long life, freedom from sickness, and immortality, and think that the gods can be persuaded to grant them these favours. But in fact this very early hierophany shows that worship does not necessarily have a self-serving agenda. People did not want anything from the sky, and knew perfectly well that they could not affect it in any way. From the very earliest times, we have experienced our world as profoundly mysterious; it holds us in an attitude of awe and wonder, which is the essence of worship. Later the people of Israel would use the word *qaddosh* to denote the sacred. It was 'separate, other'. The experience of pure transcendence was in itself profoundly satisfying. It gave people an ecstatic experience by making them aware of an existence that utterly transcended their own, and lifted them emotionally and imaginatively beyond their own limited circumstances. It was inconceivable that the sky could be 'persuaded' to do the will of poor, weak human beings.

The sky would continue to be a symbol of the sacred long after the Palaeolithic period. But a very early development showed that mythology would fail if it spoke of a reality that was too transcendent. If a myth does not enable people to participate in the sacred in some way, it becomes remote and fades from their consciousness. At some point – we do not know exactly when this happened – people in various far-flung parts of the world began to personify the sky. They started to tell stories about a 'Sky God' or

'High God', who had single-handedly created heaven and earth out of nothing. This primitive monotheism almost certainly dates back to the Palaeolithic period. Before they began to worship a number of deities, people in many parts of the world acknowledged only one Supreme God, who had created the world and governed human affairs from afar.

Nearly every pantheon has its Sky God. Anthropologists have also found Him among such tribal peoples as the Pygmies, the Australians and the Fuegians.[10] He is First Cause of all things and Ruler of heaven and earth. He is never represented by images and has no shrine or priest, because he is too exalted for a human cult. The people yearn toward their High God in prayer, believe that he is watching over them and will punish wrongdoing. Yet he is absent from their daily lives. The tribesmen say that he is inexpressible and can have no dealings with the world of men. They may turn to him in a crisis, but he is otherwise absent and is often said to have 'gone away', or 'disappeared'.

The Sky Gods of the ancient Mesopotamians, Vedic Indians, Greeks and Canaanites all dwindled in this way. In all the mythology of all these peoples, the High God is at best a shadowy, powerless figure, marginal to the divine pantheon, and more dynamic, interesting and accessible deities, such as Indra, Enlil and Baal, had come to the fore. There are stories that explain how the High God was deposed: Ouranos, the Sky God of the Greeks, for example, was actually castrated by his son Kronos, in a myth that horribly illustrates the impotence of these Creators, who were so removed from the ordinary lives of human beings that they had become peripheral. People experienced the sacred power of Baal in every rainstorm; they felt the force of Indra every time they were possessed by the transcendent fury of battle. But the old Sky Gods did not touch people's lives at all. This very early development makes it clear that mythology will not succeed if it concentrates on the supernatural; it will only remain vital if it is primarily concerned with humanity.

The fate of the Sky God reminds us of another popular misconception. It is often assumed that the early myths gave people in the pre-scientific world information about the origin of the cosmos. The story of the Sky God represented exactly this type of speculation, but the myth was a failure, because it did not touch people's ordinary lives, told them nothing about their human nature and did not help them to solve their perennial problems. The demise of the Sky Gods helps to explain why the Creator God worshipped by Jews, Christians and Muslims has disappeared from the lives of many people in the West. A myth does not impart factual information, but is primarily a guide to behaviour. Its truth will only be revealed if it is put into practice – ritually or ethically. If it is perused as though it were a purely intellectual hypothesis, it becomes remote and incredible.

The High Gods may have been demoted, but the sky never lost its power to remind people of the sacred. Height has remained a mythical symbol of the divine – a relic of Palaeolithic spirituality. In mythology and mysticism, men and women regularly reach for the sky, and devise rituals and techniques of trance and concentration that enable them to put these ascension stories into practice and 'rise' to a 'higher' state of consciousness. Sages claim that they have mounted through the various levels of the celestial world until they reach the divine sphere. Yoga practitioners are said to fly through the air; mystics levitate; prophets climb high mountains and break into a more sublime mode of being.[11] When people aspired towards the transcendence represented by the sky, they felt that they could escape from the frailty of the human condition and pass to what lies beyond. That is why mountains are so often holy in mythology: midway between heaven and earth, they were a place where men such as Moses could meet their god. Myths about flight and ascent have appeared in all cultures, expressing a universal desire for transcendence and liberation from the constraints of the human condition. These myths should not be read literally. When we read of Jesus ascending to heaven, we are not meant to imagine him whirling through the stratosphere. When the Prophet Muhammad flies from Mecca to Jerusalem and then climbs up a ladder to the Divine Throne, we are to understand that he has broken through to a new level of spiritual attainment. When the Prophet Elijah ascends to heaven in a fiery chariot, he has left the frailty of the human condition behind, and passed away into the sacred realm that lies beyond our earthly experience.

Scholars believe that the very first myths of ascent date back to the Palaeolithic period, and that they were associated with the shaman, the chief religious practitioner of hunting societies. The shaman was a master of trance and ecstasy, whose visions and dreams encapsulated the ethos of the hunt, and gave it a spiritual meaning. The hunt was highly dangerous. Hunters would leave their tribe for days at a time, would have to relinquish the security of their cave, and risk their lives to bring food back to their people. But, as we shall see, it was not merely a pragmatic enterprise, but, like all their activities, had a transcendent dimension. The shaman also embarked on a quest, but his was a spiritual expedition. It was thought that he had the power to leave his body and to travel in spirit to the celestial world. When he fell into a trance, he flew through the air and communed with the gods for the sake of his people.

In the Palaeolithic cave shrines of Lascaux in France and Altamira in Spain, we find paintings depicting the hunt; alongside the animals and the huntsmen, there are men wearing bird masks, suggestive of flight, who were probably shamans. Even today, in hunting societies from Siberia to Tierra del Fuego, shamans believe that when they go into a trance they ascend to heaven and speak with the gods, as all humans did long ago in the Golden Age. A shaman is given special training in the techniques of ecstasy. Sometimes he suffers a psychotic breakdown during his adolescence, which represents a severance from his old profane consciousness and the recovery of powers that were given to the very earliest human beings but which have now been lost. In special ritual sessions, the shaman falls into a trance to the accompaniment of drums and dancing. Often he climbs a tree or a post that symbolises the Tree, Mountain or Ladder that once linked heaven and earth.[12] A modern shaman describes his journey through the depths of the earth to heaven in this way:

When the people sing, I dance. I enter the earth.
I go in at a place like a place where people drink

water. I travel a long way, very far . . . When I emerge, I am already climbing. I'm climbing threads, the threads that lie over there in the south . . . and when you arrive at God's place, you make yourself small . . . You do what you have to do there. Then you return to where everybody is.[13]

Like the dangerous expedition of the hunter, the shaman's quest is a confrontation with death. When he returns to his community his soul is still absent from his body, and he has to be revived by colleagues, who 'take hold of your head and blow about the sides of your face. This is how you manage to be alive again. Friends, if they don't do that to you, you die . . . you just die and are dead.'[14]

Spiritual flight does not involve a physical journey, but an ecstasy in which the soul is felt to leave the body. There can be no ascent to the highest heaven without a prior descent into the depths of the earth. There can be no new life without death. The themes of this primitive spirituality would recur in the spiritual journeys undertaken by mystics and yogins in all cultures. It is highly significant that these myths and rituals of ascension go back to the earliest period of human history. It means that one of the essential yearnings of humanity is the desire to get 'above' the human state. As soon as human beings had completed the evolutionary process, they found that a longing for transcendence was built into their condition.

Shamans operate only in hunting societies, and animals play an important role in their spirituality. During his training, a modern shaman sometimes lives with animals in the wild. He is supposed to meet an animal, who will instruct him in the secrets of ecstasy, teach him animal language, and become his constant companion. This is not regarded as a regression. In hunting societies, animals are not seen as inferior beings, but have superior wisdom. They know the secrets of longevity and immortality, and, by communing with them, the shaman gains an enhanced life. In the Golden Age, before the fall, it is thought that human beings could talk with animals, and, until he has recovered this prelapsarian skill, a shaman cannot ascend to the divine world.[15] But his journey also has a practical objective. Like the hunter, he brings food to his people. In Greenland, for example, the Eskimos believe that the seals belong to a goddess, who is called the Mistress of Animals. When there is a shortage of game, the shaman is dispatched to appease her and end the famine.[16]

It is likely that the Palaeolithic peoples had similar myths and rites. It is a crucial fact that *homo sapiens* was also 'the hunter ape', who preyed on other animals, killed and ate them.[17] Palaeolithic mythology also seems to have been characterised by great reverence for the animals that men now felt compelled to kill. Humans were ill-equipped for hunting, because they were weaker and smaller than most of their prey. They had to compensate for this by developing new weapons and techniques. But more problematic was a psychological ambivalence. Anthropologists note that modern indigenous peoples frequently refer to animals or birds as 'peoples' on the same level as themselves. They tell stories about humans becoming animals and *vice versa*; to kill an animal is to kill a friend, so tribesmen often feel guilt after a successful expedition. Because it is a sacred activity and charged with such high levels of anxiety, hunting is invested with ceremonial solemnity and surrounded with rites and taboos. Before an expedition, a hunter must abstain from sex and keep himself in a state of ritual purity; after the killing, the meat is stripped from the bones, and the skeleton, skull and pelt are carefully laid out in an attempt to reconstruct the animal and give it new life.[18]

It seems that the very first hunters felt a similar ambivalence. They had to learn a hard lesson. In the pre-agricultural age, they could not grow their own food so the preservation of their own lives meant the destruction of other creatures to whom they felt closely akin. Their chief prey were the great mammals, whose bodies and facial expressions resembled their own. Hunters could see their fear and identify with their cries of terror. Their blood flowed like human blood. Faced with this potentially intolerable dilemma, they created myths and rituals that enabled them to come to terms with the murder of their fellow-creatures, some of which have survived in the mythologies of later cultures. People continued to feel unhappy about the slaughter and consumption of animals long after the Palaeolithic period. Central to almost all the religious systems of antiquity was the ritual of animal sacrifice, which preserved the old hunting ceremonies and honoured the beasts that laid down their lives for the sake of human beings.

The first great flowering of mythology, therefore, came into being at a time when *homo sapiens* became *homo necans*, 'man the killer', and found it very difficult to accept the conditions of his existence in a violent world. Mythology often springs from profound anxiety about essentially practical problems, which cannot be assuaged by purely logical arguments. Human beings had been able to compensate for their physical disadvantages by developing the rational powers of their extraordinarily large brains when they developed their hunting skills. They invented weapons, and learned how to organise their society with maximum efficiency and to work together as a team. Even at this early stage, *homo sapiens* was developing what the Greeks would call *logos*, the logical, pragmatic and scientific mode of thought that enabled them to function success-fully in the world.

Logos is quite different from mythical thinking. Unlike myth, *logos* must correspond accurately to objective facts. It is the mental activity we use when we want to make things happen in the external world: when we organise our society or develop tech-nology. Unlike myth, it is essentially pragmatic. Where myth looks back to the imaginary world of the sacred archetype or to a lost paradise, *logos* forges ahead, constantly trying to discover something new, to refine old insights, create startling inventions, and achieve a greater control over the environment. Myth and *logos* both have their limitations, however. In the pre-modern world, most people realised that myth and reason were complementary; each had its separate sphere, each its particular area of compe-tence, and human beings needed both these modes of thought. A myth could not tell a hunter how to kill his prey or how to organise an expedition effi-ciently, but it helped him to deal with his compli-cated emotions about the killing of animals. *Logos* was efficient, practical and rational, but it could not answer questions about the ultimate value of human life nor could it mitigate human pain and sorrow.[19] From the very beginning, therefore, *homo sapiens* understood instinctively that myth and *logos* had separate jobs to do. He used *logos* to develop new weaponry, and myth, with its accompanying rituals, to reconcile himself to the tragic facts of life that threatened to overwhelm him, and prevent him from acting effectively.

The extraordinary underground caverns at Altamira and Lascaux give us a tantalising glimpse of Palaeolithic spirituality.[20] The numinous paintings of deer, bison and woolly ponies, of shamans disguised as animals, and hunters with their spears, were painted with exquisite care and skill in deep subterranean caverns, which are extremely difficult of access. These grottoes were probably the very first temples and cathedrals. There has been lengthy academic discussion of the meaning of these caves; the paintings probably depict local legends that we shall never know. But certainly they set the scene for a profound meeting between men and the godlike, archetypal animals that adorn the cavern walls and ceilings. Pilgrims had to crawl through dank and dangerous underground tunnels before they reached the grottoes, burrowing ever more deeply into the heart of darkness until they finally came face to face with the painted beasts. We find here the same complex of images and ideas that inform the quest of the shaman. As in the shamanic sessions, there was probably music, dancing and singing in the caves; there was a journey to another world that began with a descent into the depths of the earth; and there was communion with animals in a magical dimension, set apart from the mundane, fallen world.

The experience would have been especially powerful for newcomers, who had never ventured into the caverns before, and it seems likely that the caves were used in initiation rites that transformed the young men of the community into hunters. Initiation ceremonies were central to the religion of the ancient world, and remain crucial in traditional societies today.[21] In tribal communities, adolescent boys are still torn away from their mothers, separated from the community, and forced to undergo an ordeal

designed to transform them into men. Like the journey of the shaman, this is a process of death and
rebirth: the boy has to die to childhood and enter
the world of adult responsibilities. Initiates are
buried in the ground, or in a tomb; they are told
that they are about to be devoured by a monster, or
killed by a spirit. They are subjected to intense physical pain and darkness; they are usually circumcised
or tattooed. The experience is so intense and traumatic that an initiate is changed forever. Psychol-
ogists tell us that this type of isolation and
deprivation not only brings about a regressive disor-
ganisation of the personality, but that, if it is properly controlled, it can promote a constructive
reorganisation of deeper forces within a person. At
the end of his ordeal, the boy has learned that death
is a new beginning. He returns to his people with a
man's body and soul. By facing up to the prospect
of imminent death, and learning that it too is only
a rite of passage to a new form of existence, he is
ready to risk his life for his people by becoming a
hunter or warrior.

It is usually during the trauma of initiation that

a neophyte hears the most sacred myths of his tribe for the first time. This is an important point. A myth is not a story that can be recited in a profane or trivial setting. Because it imparts sacred knowledge, it is always recounted in a ritualised setting that sets it apart from ordinary profane experience, and can only be understood in the solemn context of spiritual and psychological transformation.[22] Mythology is the discourse we need in extremity. We have to be prepared to allow a myth to change us forever. Together with the rituals that break down the barrier between the listener and the story, and which help him to make it his own, a mythical narrative is designed to push us beyond the safe certainties of the familiar world into the unknown. Reading a myth without the transforming ritual that goes with it is as incomplete an experience as simply reading the lyrics of an opera without the music. Unless it is encountered as part of a process of regeneration, of death and rebirth, mythology makes no sense.

Almost certainly, it was from the experience of ritual in shrines like those of Lascaux, and from the experience of the shaman and the hunt, that the myth of the hero was born. The hunter, the shaman and the neophyte all had to turn their backs on the familiar, and endure fearsome trials. They all had to face the prospect of violent death before returning with gifts to nourish the community. All cultures have developed a similar mythology about the heroic quest. The hero feels that there is something missing in his own life or in his society. The old ideas that have nourished his community for generations no longer speak to him. So he leaves home and endures death-defying adventures. He fights monsters, climbs inaccessible mountains, traverses dark forests and, in the process, dies to his old self, and gains a new insight or skill, which he brings back to his people. Prometheus stole fire from the gods for humanity, and had to endure centuries of agonising punishment; Aeneas was forced to leave his old life behind, see his homeland in flames, and descend to the underworld before he could found the new city of Rome. So engrained is the myth of the hero that even the lives of historical figures, such as the Buddha, Jesus or Muhammad, are told in a way that conforms to this archetypal pattern, which was probably first forged in the Palaeolithic era.

Again, when people told these stories about the heroes of their tribe, they were not simply hoping to entertain their listeners. The myth tells us what we have to do if we want to become a fully human person. Every single one of us has to be a hero at some time in our lives. Every baby forced through the narrow passage of the birth canal, which is not unlike the labyrinthine tunnels at Lascaux, has to leave the safety of the womb, and face the trauma of entry into a terrifyingly unfamiliar world. Every mother who gives birth, and who risks death for her child, is also heroic.[23] You cannot be a hero unless you are prepared to give up everything; there is no ascent to the heights without a prior descent into darkness, no new life without some form of death. Throughout our lives, we all find ourselves in situations in which we come face to face with the unknown, and the myth of the hero shows us how we should behave. We all have to face the final rite of passage, which is death.

Some Palaeolithic heroes survived in later mythical literature. The Greek hero Herakles, for example, is almost certainly a relic of the hunting period.[24]

He even dresses in animal skins, like a caveman, and carries a club. Herakles is a shaman, famous for his skill with animals; he visits the underworld, seeks the fruit of immortality, and ascends to the realm of the gods on Mount Olympus. Again, the Greek goddess Artemis, known as the 'Mistress of Animals',[25] a huntress and the patron of untamed nature, may also be a Palaeolithic figure.[26]

Hunting was an exclusively male activity, and yet one of the most powerful hunters in the Palaeolithic era was female. The earliest of the small figurines depicting a pregnant woman, which have been found throughout Africa, Europe and the Middle East, date from this period. Artemis is simply one embodiment of the Great Goddess, a fearsome deity who was not only the Mistress of Animals, but the source of life. She is no nurturing earth mother, however, but is implacable, vengeful and demanding. Artemis herself is notorious in exacting sacrifice and bloodshed, if the rituals of the hunt are violated. This formidable goddess also survived the Palaeolithic era. At the town of Catal Huyuk in Turkey, which dates from the seventh or sixth millennium, for example, archaeologists have unearthed large stone reliefs of the goddess in the act of giving birth. She is sometimes flanked by animals, bulls' horns or the skulls of boars – relics of a successful hunt, and also symbols of the male.

Why should a goddess have become so dominant in an aggressively male society? This may be due to an unconscious resentment of the female. The goddess of Catal Huyuk gives birth eternally, but her partner, the bull, must die. Hunters risked their lives to support their women and children. The guilt and anxiety induced by hunting, combined with frustration resulting from ritual celibacy, could have been projected onto the image of a powerful woman, who demands endless bloodshed.[27] The hunters could see that women were the source of new life; it was they – not the expendable males – who ensured the continuity of the tribe. The female thus became an awe-inspiring icon of life itself – a life that required the ceaseless sacrifice of men and animals.

These fragmentary glimpses of our Palaeolithic past show that mythology was no self-indulgent panacea. It forced men and women to confront the inexorable realities of life and death. Human beings had a tragic vision. They longed to scale the heavens, yet they realised that they could only do this if they faced up to their mortality, left the safe world behind, descended into the depths, and died to their old selves. Mythology and its accompanying rituals helped Palaeolithic people to move from one stage of life to another, in such a way that when death finally came it was seen as the last and final initiation to another, totally unknown mode of being. This early insight was never lost, but continued to guide men and women when they embarked on the next great revolution of human history.

The Neolithic Period: The Mythology of the Farmers (*c.* 8000 to 4000 BCE)

About ten thousand years ago, human beings invented agriculture. Hunting was no longer their chief source of food, because they discovered that the earth was an apparently inexhaustible source of nourishment. There have been few developments that have been more important for the human race than the agrarian Neolithic revolution. We can sense the awe, delight and terror of these pioneering farmers in the mythology they developed as they adapted to their new circumstances, fragments of which were preserved in the mythical narratives of later cultures. Agriculture was the product of *logos* but, unlike the technological revolutions of our own day, it was not regarded as a purely secular enterprise. It led to a great spiritual awakening that gave people an entirely new understanding of themselves and their world.

The new science of agriculture was approached with religious awe.[28] The people of the Palaeolithic period had regarded hunting as a sacred act and now farming also became sacramental. When they tilled the fields or gathered the harvest, the farmers had to be in a state of ritual purity. As they watched the seeds descending into the depths of the earth, and realised that they broke open in the darkness to bring forth a marvellously different form of life, planters recognised a hidden force at work. The crop was an epiphany, a revelation of divine energy, and when farmers cultivated the land and brought forth food for their community, they felt that they had entered a sacred realm and participated in this miraculous abundance.[29] The earth seemed to sustain all creatures – plants, animals and humans – as in a living womb.

Rituals were designed to replenish this power lest it exhaust itself. So the first seeds were 'thrown away' as offerings, and the first fruits of the harvest were left unpicked, as a way of recycling these sacred energies. There is even evidence that in Central America, parts of Africa, the Pacific Islands and Dravidian India, human beings were offered in sacrifice. Two principles lay at the heart of these rites. First, you could not expect to get something for nothing; in order to receive, you had to give something back. Second was a holistic vision of reality. The sacred was not felt to be a metaphysical reality, beyond the natural world. It could only be encountered in the earth and its products, which were themselves sacred. Gods, human beings, animals and plants all shared the same nature, and could, therefore, invigorate and replenish one another.

Human sexuality, for example, was regarded as essentially the same as the divine force that fructified the earth. In early Neolithic mythology, the harvest was seen as the fruit of a hierogamy, a sacred marriage: the soil was female; the seeds divine semen; and rain the sexual congress of heaven and earth. It was common for men and women to engage in ritual sex when they planted their crops. Their own intercourse, itself a sacred act, would activate the creative energies of the soil, just as the farmer's spade or plough was a sacred phallus that opened the womb of the earth and made it big with seed. The Bible shows that these ritualised orgies were practised in ancient Israel well into the sixth century BCE, to the fury of such prophets as Hosea and Ezekiel. Even in the Jerusalem temple there were ceremonies in honour of Asherah, the fertility goddess of Canaan, and a house of sacred prostitutes.[30]

In the early stages of the Neolithic revolution, however, the earth was not always regarded as female.[31] In China and Japan the ground of being was neuter and only later, probably as a result of the maternal role of women in family life, did the earth take on a female, nurturing character. In other parts of the world the earth was not personified, but was venerated as sacred in herself. She produced all things from her womb in the same way as a woman gave birth to a child. Some of the earliest creation myths in Europe and North America imagined the first humans emerging from the earth like plants: like seeds, their lives began in the underworld until the new people climbed to the surface, or sprouted like flowers and were collected by their human mothers.[32] Where once people had imagined themselves ascending to the heights in order to encounter the divine, they now made ritual contact with the sacred in the earth. Neolithic labyrinths have been discovered that are similar to the Palaeolithic tunnels at Lascaux but, instead of going to meet the sacred animals in the underground caverns, these worshippers felt that they were entering the womb of Mother Earth, and making a mystical return to the source of all being.[33]

These creation myths taught people that they belong to the earth in the same way as the rocks, rivers and trees do. They must, therefore, respect her natural rhythms. Others expressed a profound identification with a place, a bond that was deeper than that of family or paternity. This kind of myth was especially popular in ancient Greece. Erechthonius, the fifth mythical king of Athens, was born from the sacred soil of the Acropolis, a sacred event commemorated from a very early date in a special shrine.

The Neolithic revolution had made people aware of a creative energy that pervaded the entire cosmos. It was at first an undifferentiated sacred force, which made the earth herself a manifestation of the divine. But the mythical imagination always becomes more concrete and circumstantial; what was originally amorphous gains definition and becomes particular. Just as the veneration of the sky had led to the personification of the Sky God, the maternal, nurturing earth became the Mother Goddess. In Syria, she was identified as Asherah, consort of El, the High God, or as Anat, El's daughter; in Sumer in Mesopotamia, she was called Inanna; in Egypt, Isis; and in Greece she became Hera, Demeter and Aphrodite. The Mother Goddess fused with the Great Mother of the hunting societies, retaining many of her frightening characteristics. Anat, for example, is a ruthless warrior, and often depicted wading through an ocean of blood; Demeter is described as furious and vengeful, and even Aphrodite, goddess of love, exacts fearful revenge.

Again, mythology is not escapist. The new Neolithic myths continued to force people to face up to the reality of death. They were not pastoral idylls, and the Mother Goddess was not a gentle, consoling deity, because agriculture was not experienced as a peaceful, contemplative occupation. It was a constant battle, a desperate struggle, against sterility, drought, famine and the violent forces of nature, which were also manifestations of sacred power.[34] The sexual imagery of planting did not mean that people experienced agriculture as a romantic love affair with nature. Human reproduction was itself highly dangerous for mother and child. In the same way, tilling the fields was accomplished only after hard, backbreaking labour. In the book of Genesis, the loss of the primordial paradisal state is experienced as a falling into agriculture. In Eden, the first human beings had tended God's garden effortlessly. After the Fall, the woman brings forth her children in sorrow, and the man has to wrest a living from the soil by the sweat of his brow. [35]

In the early mythology, farming is pervaded by violence, and food is produced only by a constant warfare against the sacred forces of death and destruction. The seed has to go down into the earth and die in order to bring forth its fruit, and its death is painful and traumatic. Farming implements look like weapons, corn must be ground to powder, and grapes trampled to unrecognisable pulp before they can become wine. We see all this in the myths about the Mother Goddess, whose consorts are nearly all torn apart, dismembered, brutally mutilated, and killed before they can rise again, with the crops, to new life. All these myths speak of a struggle to the death. In the old heroic myths dating from the Palaeolithic age, it was usually a male hero who set forth on a dangerous journey to bring help to his people. After the Neolithic revolution, the males are often helpless and passive. It is the female goddess who wanders through the world on a quest, who struggles with death, and brings nourishment to the human race. The Earth Mother becomes a symbol of female heroism, in myths that speak ultimately of balance and restored harmony.

This is clear in the myth of Anat, the sister and spouse of Baal, the storm god, which symbolises not only the struggle of farming but also the difficulty of attaining wholeness and harmony. Baal, who brings rain to the parched earth, is himself engaged in a constant creative battle with monsters, the forces of chaos and disintegration. One day, however, he is attacked by Mot, the god of death, sterility and drought, who constantly threatens to turn the earth into a desolate wilderness. At Mot's approach, Baal

for once is overcome with fear, and surrenders without resistance. Mot chews him up, like a tasty morsel
of lamb, and forces him down into the underworld,
the land of the dead. Because Baal can no longer
bring rain to the earth, vegetation withers and dies,
amidst general lamentation. El, Baal's father – a typical High God – is helpless. When he hears of Baal's
death, he comes down from his high throne, puts on
sackcloth, and gashes his cheeks in the traditional
rites of mourning, but cannot save his son. The only
effective deity is Anat. Filled with grief and rage,
she wanders through the earth, distraught, searching for her *alter ego*, her other half. The Syrian text
which has preserved this myth tells us that she yearns
for Baal 'as a cow her calf or a ewe her lamb'.[36] The
Mother Goddess is as fierce and beyond control as
an animal when its young is in danger. When Anat
finds Baal's remains, she makes a great funeral
banquet in his honour, and, uttering a passionate
complaint to El, she continues her search for Mot.
When she finds him, she cleaves Mot in two with a
ritual sickle, winnows him in a sieve, scorches him,
grinds him in a mill, and scatters his flesh over the

fields, treating him in exactly the same way as a farmer treats his grain.

Our sources are incomplete, so we do not know how Anat managed to bring Baal back to life. But both Baal and Mot are divine, so neither can be wholly extinguished. The battle between the two will continue, and the harvest will only be produced each year in the teeth of death. In one version of the myth, Anat restores Baal so completely that the next time Mot attacks him, he responds much more vigorously. Rain returns to the earth, the valleys run with honey, and the heavens rain down precious oil. The story ends with the sexual reunion of Baal and Anat, an image of wholeness and completion, cultically re-enacted during the New Year's festival.

We find much the same pattern in Egypt, though Isis is less powerful than Anat. Osiris, the first king of Egypt, teaches his people the science of agriculture. His brother Seth, who aspires to the throne, assassinates him, and Isis, his sister and spouse, roams the world, searching for his body. When she finds the corpse, she can only revive him long enough to enable him to conceive Horus, a son to continue his line, before he expires again. Then Osiris's body is cut into pieces, and each fragment is buried, like seed, in a different place throughout Egypt. He becomes the ruler of Duat, the world of the dead, and is also responsible each year for the annual harvest, his death and dismemberment ritually enacted alongside the cutting and threshing of the crops. The god of the dead is often also the god of the harvest, showing that life and death are inextricably entwined. You cannot have one without the other. The god who dies and comes to life again epitomises a universal process, like the waxing and waning of the seasons. There may be new life, but the central feature of the myth and the cult of these dying vegetation gods is always the catastrophe and bloodshed, and the victory of the forces of life is never complete.

This becomes especially clear in the myth that recounts the descent of the Mesopotamian goddess Inanna into the underworld. It can be read as another initiation ceremony in the nether regions, an experience of death that leads to new life. Inanna has no benevolent motive for her dangerous journey into the depths of the earth. As far as we can tell from our sources, which are incomplete, her purpose is to usurp her sister Ereshkigal, Queen of Hell, who is also Mistress of Life. Before she can enter Ereshkigal's lapis lazuli palace, Inanna has to pass through the seven gates of her sister's city's seven walls. Each time, the gatekeeper challenges Inanna, and forces her to shed an item of clothing, so that when she finally enters her sister's presence, Inanna is stripped of all her defences. Her attempted coup fails, the Seven Judges of the underworld sentence Inanna to death, and her corpse is displayed on a spike.

Inanna is, however, rescued by the other gods, and her return to earth, accompanied by a horde of devils, is triumphant and terrible. When she arrives home, she finds that her husband, the handsome young shepherd Dumuzi, has dared to sit upon her throne. Enraged, Inanna passes the sentence of death upon him, Dumuzi flees, pursued by devils who force him down into the underworld to take Inanna's place, but a deal is made, whereby the year is divided between Dumuzi and his sister Geshtinanna, each passing six months with Ereshkigal in the underworld. But the world is changed forever by Inanna's adventure, since the absence of Dumuzi, now god of vegetation, causes seasonal change. When he returns to Inanna, the earth comes to life with the birth of lambs, and the shooting of the grain, quickly followed by the harvest. When he goes down into the underworld, the earth suffers the long drought of summer. There is no final victory over death. The Sumerian poem that recounts the myth ends with the cry: 'O Ereshkigal! Great is your praise!'[37] What remains most poignantly in the mind is the lament of the women, especially of Dumuzi's mother, when she mourns the loss of her son, 'desolate in a desolate place; where once he was alive, now he lies like a young bull felled to the ground'.[38]

This Mother Goddess is not a redeemer, but the cause of death and sorrow. Her journey is an initiation, a rite of transformation that is required of us all. Inanna goes down into the world of death, to meet her sister, a buried and unsuspected aspect of her own being. Ereshkigal represents the ultimate reality. In many myths, dating originally from this period, a meeting with the Mother Goddess represents the ultimate adventure of the hero, the supreme illumination. Mistress of life and death, Ereshkigal too is a Mother Goddess, depicted as constantly giving birth. In order to approach her, and gain true insight, Inanna has to lay aside the clothes that protect her vulnerability, dismantle her egotism, die to her old self, assimilate what seems opposed and inimical to her, and accept the intolerable: namely, that there can be no life without death, darkness and deprivation.[39]

The rituals associated with Inanna concentrated on the tragedy of her story and never celebrated her reunion with Dumuzi in the springtime. Because it so powerfully represented what was experienced as a fundamental law of existence, the cult was widespread. Inanna was called Ishtar by the Babylonians, and Astarte (or Asherah) in Syria; in the Near East, Dumuzi was known as Tammuz, and his death was lamented by the women of the region.[40] In Greece, he was called Adonis, because the women in the Semitic world mourned the loss of their 'lord' (*adon*). The story of Adonis changed over the years, but in its original form, it conformed to the basic structure of the Sumerian myth, for it shows the goddess handing her young consort over to death.[41] Like the Great Goddess of the hunters, the Neolithic Mother Goddess shows that, though men may seem to be more powerful, it is really the female which is the stronger and in control.

This is also apparent in the Greek myth of Demeter and her daughter, Persephone, which almost certainly dates back to the Neolithic period.[42] Demeter is the Grain Mother who protects the crops and the fruitfulness of the earth. When Hades, ruler of the underworld, abducts Persephone, Demeter leaves Mount Olympus and wanders grief-stricken through the world. In her rage, she withholds the harvest, threatening to starve human beings, unless her daughter Kore ('the girl') is returned. In alarm, Zeus sends Hermes, the divine messenger, to rescue Kore, but unfortunately she has eaten some pomegranate seeds during her time in the Nether World, and is therefore obliged to spend four months of the year with Hades, now her husband. When she is reunited with her mother, Demeter lifts the ban, and the earth becomes fruitful once again.

This is not a simple nature allegory. The rites of Demeter did not coincide with either the sowing or the harvest. Persephone may descend into the earth, like a seed, but in the Mediterranean a seed takes only a few weeks to germinate, not four months. Like the myth of Inanna, this is another story of a goddess who disappears and returns. It is a myth about death. In ancient Greece, Demeter, the grain goddess, is also Mistress of the Dead, and presides over the mystery cult at Eleusis, near Athens. These were secret rites, but it seems that they compelled the *mystai* ('initiates') to accept the inevitability of death as an essential part of life, and find that it had thereby lost its terror. The powerful rites impressed the meaning of the myth indelibly on the minds and hearts of those who went through this lengthy initiation. There is no possibility of a final victory over death. Kore has to alternate perpetually between the upper and lower worlds. There can be no grain, no food and no life, without the symbolic death of the maiden.

We know very little about the Eleusinian mysteries, but those who took part in these rites would have been puzzled if they had been asked whether they believed that Persephone really *had* descended into the earth, in the way that the myth described. The myth was true, because wherever you looked you saw that life and death were inseparable, and that the earth died and came to life again. Death was fearful, frightening and inevitable, but it was not the end. If you cut a plant, and threw away the dead branch, it gained a new sprout. Agriculture led to a new, if qualified, optimism.[43] The seed had to die, in order to produce grain; pruning was actually helpful to plants, and encouraged new growth. The initiation at Eleusis showed that the confrontation with death led to spiritual regeneration, and was a form of human pruning. It could not bring immortality – only the gods lived forever – but it could enable you to live more fearlessly and therefore more fully here on earth, looking death calmly in the face. Indeed, every day we are forced to die to the self we have already achieved. In the Neolithic period too, the myths and rituals of passage helped people to accept their mortality, to pass on to the next stage, and to have the courage to change and grow.

The Early Civilisations
(*c.* 4000 to 800 BCE)

In about 4000 BCE, human beings took another major
step forward when they began to build cities, first
in Mesopotamia and Egypt in about 4000 BCE, and
later in China, India and Crete. Some of these early
civilisations disappeared almost without trace, but
in the Fertile Crescent, in what is now Iraq, we see
an early response to the challenge of urbanisation in
the mythology that celebrated city life. Human life
was becoming more self-conscious. People could now
give permanent expression to their aspirations in the
civilised arts, and the invention of writing meant
that they could give enduring literary expression to
their mythology. They had now entered the historical age: in the cities, the rate of change accelerated,
and people became more aware of the chain of cause
and effect. The new technology gave city-dwellers a
more complete control over their environment, and

they were becoming increasingly more distinct from the natural world. It was a time of excitement, liberation and pride.

But major change on this scale also inspires great fear. It has been said that history is a process of annihilation, since each new development requires the destruction of what has gone before.[44] This was clearly the case in the Mesopotamian cities, where the mudbrick buildings needed constant maintenance and periodic reconstruction. New structures were erected on top of the levelled ruins of their predecessors, and the process of decay and renewal was thus built into the new art of town planning.[45] Civilisation was experienced as magnificent but fragile; a city shot up and flourished dramatically, but then all too quickly went into decline. When one city-state rose to pre-eminence, it preyed upon its rivals. There were wars, massacres, revolutions and deportations. The destruction meant that the culture that had been so painfully achieved needed to be rebuilt and established again and again. There was constant fear that life would revert to the old barbarism. With mingled apprehension and hope, the new urban myths meditated on the endless struggle between order and chaos.

Not surprisingly, some saw civilisation as a disaster. The biblical writers saw it as a sign of the separation from God that had followed the expulsion from Eden. Urban life seemed inherently violent, involving killing and exploitation. The first man to build a city was Cain, the first murderer,[46] his descendants invented the civilised arts: Jubal was 'the ancestor of all those who play the lyre and the pipes', and Tubal-cain 'made all kinds of bronze and iron tools'.[47] The great ziggurat or temple-tower of Babylon made a profound and unfavourable impression on the ancient Israelites. It seemed the epitome of pagan hubris, motivated solely by a desire for self-aggrandisement. They called it the Tower of Bavel or Babble, because, to punish the builders, God had 'baffled the language of all the earth-folk, and from there scattered them over the face of all the earth'.[48]

But the people of Mesopotamia themselves saw the city as a place where they could encounter the divine. It was – almost – a recreation of the lost paradise. The ziggurat replaced the mountain at the centre of the world, which had enabled the first human beings to climb up to the world of the gods. The gods lived in the cities, side by side with men and women in temples that were replicas of their palaces in the divine world. In the ancient world, every city was a holy city. As their ancestors had regarded hunting and farming as sacred and sacramental activities, these early city-dwellers saw their cultural attainments as essentially divine. In Mesopotamia, the gods had taught men how to build the ziggurats, and Enki, god of wisdom, was the patron of leather-workers, metal-smiths, barbers, builders, potters, irrigation technicians, physicians, musicians and scribes.[49] They knew that they had embarked on a wondrous enterprise that would transform human life forever; their cities were transcendent, because they went beyond anything known before. They partook of the divine creativity of the gods, who had somehow brought order out of the confusion of chaos.

But the Israelites were wrong to imagine that the people of Mesopotamia were guilty of hubris. They knew that human life – even in their imposing cities –

was flawed and transitory, in comparison with the world of the gods, which still formed the backdrop of their daily lives. Their cities were only a pale shadow of the lost paradise of Dilmun, inhabited now only by gods and a few exceptional human beings. They were acutely aware that, like human life itself, civilisation was fragile and impermanent. In Egypt, a compact country, isolated and protected from hostile forces by mountains, and fertilised by the regular flooding of the Nile, there was greater confidence in human achievement. But in Mesopotamia, where the flooding of the Tigris and Euphrates was unpredictable and often destructive, where torrential rain could turn the soil into a quagmire, or scorching winds reduce it to dust, and where there was constant threat of invasion, life was far less secure. The maintenance of civilisation seemed to require a heroic effort against the wilful and destructive powers of nature. These fears are especially evident in their flood myths. Rivers in Mesopotamia are prone to sudden shifts of direction because there are no natural obstacles, so flooding was frequent and often disastrous. A flood was not a blessing, as in

Egypt, but became a metaphor for political and social dissolution.

Whenever they enter a new era of history, people change their ideas of both humanity and divinity. In these early civilisations, men and women were becoming more like us moderns, more aware than ever before that they were the masters of their own destiny. Consequently, they could no longer see the gods in the same way as their ancestors had. Because human actions were now centre-stage, the gods seemed more remote; they were no longer a reality that was self-evident and only just out of reach. The new urban mythology saw the Flood as marking a crisis in divine–human relations. In *Atrahasis*, the longest of the Mesopotamian Flood poems, the gods, like men, are town planners. The lesser deities go on strike, exhausted by the endless labour of digging irrigation canals to make the countryside habitable, so the Mother Goddess creates human beings to perform these menial tasks instead. But they become too numerous and so noisy that Enlil, the storm god, who is kept awake by the din, decides to inundate the world as a brutal method of population control.

But Enki wants to save Atrahasis,[50] the 'exceedingly wise man' of the city of Shuruppak. The two enjoy a special friendship, so Enki tells Atrahasis to build a boat, instructing him about the technology that would keep it watertight and, because of this divine intervention, Atrahasis, like Noah, is able to save his family and the seeds of all living things. But after the waters subside, the gods are horrified by the devastation. In Mesopotamian myth, the Flood marks the beginning of the gods' withdrawal from the world. Enki takes Atrahasis and his wife to Dilmun. They would be the only humans to enjoy immortality and the old intimacy with the gods. But the story also celebrates the divinely inspired technology that had saved the human race from extinction. Increasingly in Mesopotamia, as in our own modernity, civilisation and culture would become the focus of myth and aspiration.

But the Mesopotamians were not entirely like us. The gods may have withdrawn, but people remained highly conscious of a transcendent element in their daily activities. Each city was regarded as the earthly estate of one of the gods, and every citizen – from the ruler to the humblest manual worker – was in the employ of the patron deity – of Enlil, Enki or Inanna.[51] People still adhered to the perennial philosophy, which saw everything on earth as the replica of a celestial reality. An assembly of elders ruled the city-states, so the Mesopotamians believed that a Divine Assembly of leading deities also ruled the gods. They also assumed that, just as their urban culture had developed from small agricultural communities, closely involved with the natural rhythms of the countryside, the gods had been through a similar evolution.

Hence the creation myth that has survived in the Babylonian epic known, from its opening words, as the *Enuma Elish*. Our text dates only from the first half of the second millennium BCE, but it contains much earlier material.[52] The poem begins with a theogony that shows how the gods themselves first came into being. There is no creation *ex nihilo*, but an evolutionary process, in which the first deities emerged from sacred primal matter, a sloppy, undefined substance, where everything lacks identity. Salt and bitter waters mingled together, there was no

separation of sky, earth or sea; and the gods themselves were 'nameless, natureless, futureless'.[53] The
first deities to emerge from the slime were inseparable from the elements. Apsu was the sweet river
water, Tiamat the salty sea and Mummu a misty
cloud. Their names can also be translated: 'abyss',
'void' and 'bottomless pit'.

These primal deities are still shapeless and inert.
But other gods emanate from them in couples, each
pair more clearly defined than the last. An ordered
cosmos comes into being, as these divine elements
separate from each other. First comes silt (water and
soil mixed together), represented by Lahmu and
Lahamu. Then Ansher and Kishar (the horizons of
sky and sea), and finally the Sky God, Anu, and Ea,
the earth. But this theogonic myth is not a purely
metaphysical speculation about the evolution of divinity; it is also and crucially a meditation upon
Mesopotamia, which is an alluvial region built upon
deposits of silt. Again, the divine is an aspect of the
human world. The gods are inseparable from the landscape, and in Eridu, one of the oldest of the
Mesopotamian cities, the swampy lagoon that had

made the settlement viable and surrounded the cult centre, was called the *apsu*. The myth also expressed the gradual separation from nature which the new city-dwellers were themselves experiencing.

The new gods were more active and they were able to overcome their parents: Apsu sinks into the ground, and Ea and Anu build their own palace, complete with chapels and council halls, on his prone carcass. City-building always marks peak moments of Mesopotamian cosmology. But Tiamat is still a lurking danger, and has created a mighty horde of monsters to avenge Apsu. The only god who can defeat her in pitched battle is Marduk, the splendid son of Ea. After a desperate struggle, Marduk stands on Tiamat's massive corpse, and splits it in half like a giant shellfish, to create the heaven and earth that will be inhabited by human beings. He promulgates laws and establishes a Divine Assembly to consolidate the new cosmic order. Finally, almost as an afterthought, Marduk creates the first man by mixing the blood of one of the defeated gods with a handful of dust, showing that the gods are not sealed off into a supernatural realm of their own, but that humanity and the natural world are all made up from the same divine stuff.

The myth examines the human process of change, which is at one with the development of the gods. It reflects the evolution of the Mesopotamian city-state, which had turned its back on the old agrarian society (now seen as undeveloped and sluggish), and had established itself by military force. After his victory, Marduk founds Babylon. In the centre of the city is the ziggurat of Esagila, a copy of Marduk's shrine in the divine world. As the 'symbol of infinite heaven', towering above all the other buildings, it becomes the gods' earthly home. The city is called '*bab-ilani*' (the 'gate of the gods'), the place where the divine enters the world of men. In Esagila, the gods sit down to celebrate the sacred liturgy 'from which the universe receives its structure, the hidden world is made plain and the gods assigned their places in the universe'.[54] The city could thus replace the old *axis mundi*, which had linked heaven and earth in the Golden Age.

The Bible also preserves creation myths that show Yahweh bringing the world into being by killing a sea monster, like Tiamat.[55] This type of cosmogony was popular with Middle Eastern peoples. It expressed their conviction that civilisation was an ongoing struggle, a massive effort against over-whelming odds to halt the slide back to formless barbarism. The *Enuma Elish* was chanted on the fourth day of the New Year festival. Like any myth-ical narrative, it described a mysterious and ineff-able event that had happened in the Sacred Time of 'everywhen'. It was not like an ordinary historical incident, which was over and done with. The creation of the world was a continuous process; the divine battle against chaos was still going on, and human beings needed an influx of the divine energies that held disorder and disaster at bay.

In the ancient world, a symbol became insepara-ble from its unseen referent. Because likeness consti-tutes some kind of identity, it makes that invisible reality present. The symbolic ritual of the New Year festival was a drama, which, like any good theatrical event, abolished barriers of time and place and snatched audience and participants away from their mundane preoccupations. It was a game of sacred make-believe. Worshippers felt that they had been pitched into the timeless divine realm that formed the backdrop of their daily lives. A scapegoat was killed to cancel the enervated dying year; a mock-battle re-presented Marduk's struggle against Tiamat; and a saturnalia recreated the forces of chaos, by humiliating the ruler and enthroning a carnival king in his stead. This ritualised dissolution recalls the psychic breakdown that the shaman experienced during his initiation, and the carefully orchestrated regression of the rites of passage. In archaic spirituality, a symbolic return to primordial chaos is indispensable to any new creation.[56]

As we know, a creation story never provided people with factual information about the origins of life. In the ancient world, a cosmogony was usually recited in a liturgical setting, and during a period of extremity when people felt they needed an infusion of divine energy: when they were looking into the unknown at the start of a new venture – at New Year, at a wedding or a coronation. Its purpose was not to inform but was primarily therapeutic. People would listen to the recitation of a cosmological myth when they faced impending disaster, when they wanted to bring a conflict to an end, or to heal the sick. The idea was to tap into the timeless energies that supported human existence. The myth and its accompanying rituals were a reminder that often things had to get worse before they could get better, and that survival and creativity required a dedicated struggle.

Other cosmologies pointed out that true creativity demanded self-sacrifice. In Indian Vedic mythology, creation had been the result of an act of self-immolation. Purusha, a cosmic giant, had offered himself up to the gods, who had sacrificed and dismembered him; the cosmos and the social classes that made up human society had been formed from his body, and were therefore sacred and absolute. In China, there was a popular myth about another giant, called Pan Gu, who laboured for 36,000 years to bring a viable universe into being, and then died, exhausted by the effort. The motif is also present in the Middle Eastern combat myths. Tiamat, Mot and Leviathan are not evil, but are simply fulfilling their cosmic role. They have to die and endure dismemberment before an ordered cosmos can emerge from chaos. Survival and civilised society depends upon the death and destruction of others and neither gods nor men can be truly creative, unless they are prepared to give themselves away.

Hitherto mythology had centred almost entirely on the primordial feats and struggles of the gods or the archetypal ancestors of primordial time. But the urban myths began to impinge upon the historical world. Because there was now greater reliance upon human ingenuity, people began to see themselves as independent agents. Their own activities came to the foreground, and, increasingly, the gods seemed more distant. Poets began to reinterpret the old stories. We can see this development in the Babylonian poem known as *The Epic of Gilgamesh*. Gilgamesh was probably a historical figure, who lived in about 2600 BCE: he is listed in the records as the fifth king of Uruk in southern Mesopotamia and later became a folk hero. The earliest legends recount his adventures with his servant Enkidu. They include typical heroic and shamanic feats, such as fighting with monsters, visiting the underworld, and conversing with the goddess. Later these stories were given deeper meaning, and became a quest for eternal life. But in the final version of the poem, written in about 1300 BCE, the myth explores the limits and meaning of human culture.

At the beginning of the poem, we see Gilgamesh as a man who has lost his way. There is a storm in his heart, and he has begun to terrorise his people, who plead with the gods for redress. But, significantly, the gods are no longer willing to intervene directly in human affairs, and act through an intermediary instead. To give Gilgamesh something serious to contend with, they create Enkidu, a wild, primitive man who runs amok in the countryside. His body covered in a shaggy pelt, wild-haired, naked, eating grass, and drinking pond-water, Enkidu is 'Man-as-he-was-in-the-beginning',[57] who is more at home with animals than human beings. To tame Enkidu, Gilgamesh sends the prostitute Shamhat to teach him civilised ways. After six nights with Shamhat, Enkidu finds that his bond with the natural, animal world has been broken. He has become civilised, but this involves loss as well as gain. Enkidu has been 'diminished', but also has become 'profound', and 'like a god'.[58] He has acquired the wisdom and refinement that will enable him to enjoy the sophisticated lifestyle of Uruk, which is so far beyond the natural state of humanity that it seems divine.

Gilgamesh and Enkidu become friends, and set off on their adventures. In the course of their wanderings, they meet Ishtar. In the older mythology, marriage with the Mother Goddess had often represented the supreme enlightenment and the climax of a hero's quest, but Gilgamesh turns Ishtar down. It is a powerful critique of the traditional mythology, which can no longer speak fully to urban men and women. Gilgamesh does not see civilisation as a divine enterprise. Ishtar is a destroyer of culture: she is like a water skin that soaks its carrier, a shoe that pinches its wearer, and a door that cannot keep out the wind.[59] None of her relationships has lasted; she has ruined each one of her lovers.[60] Mortals are better off without these destructive encounters with irresponsible gods. Gilgamesh, the civilised man, declares his independence of the divine. It is better for gods and humans to go their separate ways.

Ishtar takes her revenge, and Enkidu sickens and dies. Gilgamesh is distraught. Oppressed by the realisation that he himself must die, he recalls that the survivor of the Flood – in this poem called Utnapishtim – was granted eternal life, and sets off to visit him in Dilmun. But human beings cannot revert to primitive spirituality and this quest for the world of the gods represents a cultural regression; Gilgamesh roams over the steppes, unshaven, wildhaired, and clad only in a lion's skin. Like a shaman, he follows the course of the sun through uninhabited lands, has a vision of the underworld, and seeks a 'secret knowledge of the gods'.[61] When he finally reaches Dilmun, however, Utnapishtim explains that the gods will no longer suspend the laws of nature for favoured humans. The old myths can no longer serve as a guide for human aspiration. The visit to Dilmun reverses the old mythical approach.[62] In *Atrahasis*, the story of the Flood was told from the gods' point of view, but here Utnapishtim reflects on his own experiences, on the practical difficulties of launching his boat, and on his own human reaction to the devastation wrought by the Flood. Where the old myths had concentrated on the sacred world and not been much concerned with temporal events and figures, here the historical Gilgamesh visits the mythical Utnapishtim. History was beginning to impinge upon mythology, as the gods had begun their retreat from the human world.[63]

Instead of getting privileged information from the gods, Gilgamesh receives a painful lesson on the limitations of humanity. He heads back to civilisation: bathes, throws away his lion skin, dresses his hair and dons clean clothes. Henceforth, he will concentrate on building the walls of Uruk, and cultivating the civilised arts. He personally will die, but these monuments will be his immortality, especially the invention of writing, which will record his achievements for posterity.[64] Where Utnapishtim had become wise by speaking with a god, Gilgamesh has learned to reflect upon his own experience without divine aid. He has lost some illusions, but gained 'complete wisdom', returning 'weary but at last resigned'.[65] He has fallen away from the ancient mythical vision, but history has its own consolations.

There was a similar re-evaluation of the old

mythical ideals in Greece. The myth of Adonis, for example, recast the story of Dumuzi and Ishtar, and transformed it into a political myth.[66] Adonis is incapable of citizenship. A hopeless hunter, he would have failed the initiation rites that turned Greek adolescents into citizens, which often centred on hunting ordeals. In thrall to two goddesses, he never separates from the world of women. Greek citizens were united to the *polis* through the family, but Adonis is the child of incest, an act that perverts the family ideal, and fails to found a family of his own. His irresponsible lifestyle is closer to Tyranny, a form of government which put the king above the law, and which the Athenians had discarded. Adonis's festival, characterised by the unbridled lamentations of the women, was regarded with distaste by the male establishment. He was, in short, politically retarded, and may have helped Athenians to define themselves by personifying everything that is opposed to the sober, male ethos of the *polis*.

Urban life had changed mythology. The gods were beginning to seem remote. Increasingly the old rituals and stories failed to project men and women into the divine realm, which had once seemed so close. People were becoming disillusioned with the old mythical vision that had nourished their ancestors. As cities became more organised, policing more efficient, and robbers and bandits brought to justice, the gods seemed increasingly careless and indifferent to the plight of humanity. There was a spiritual vacuum. In some parts of the civilised world, the old spirituality declined and nothing new appeared to take its place. Eventually this malaise led to yet another great transformation.

The Axial Age (*c.* 800 to 200 BCE)

By the eighth century BCE, the malaise was becoming more widespread, and in four distinct regions an impressive array of prophets and sages began to seek a new solution. The German philosopher Karl Jaspers called this period the 'Axial Age' because it proved to be pivotal in the spiritual development of humanity; the insights gained during this time have continued to nourish men and women to the present day.[67] It marks the beginning of religion as we know it. People became conscious of their nature, their situation and their limitations with unprecedented clarity. New religious and philosophical systems emerged: Confucianism and Taoism in China; Buddhism and Hinduism in India; monotheism in the Middle East and Greek rationalism in Europe. These Axial traditions were associated with such men as the great Hebrew prophets of the eighth, seventh and sixth centuries; with the sages of the *Upanishads*, and the Buddha (*c.* 563–483) in India; with

Confucius (551–479) and the author of the *Dao De Jing* in China;[68] and with the fifth-century tragedians, Socrates (469–399), Plato (*c.* 427–347) and Aristotle (*c.* 384–322 BCE) in Greece.

There is much about the Axial Age that remains mysterious. We do not know why it involved only the Chinese, Indians, Greeks and Jews, and why nothing comparable developed in Mesopotamia or Egypt. It is certainly true that the Axial regions were all caught up in political, social and economic upheaval. There were wars, deportations, massacres and destruction of cities. A new market economy was also developing: power was passing from priests and kings to merchants, and this disturbed the old hierarchies. All these new faiths developed not in remote deserts or mountain hermitages, but in an environment of capitalism and high finance. But this upheaval cannot fully explain the Axial revolution, which made an indelible impression on the way that human beings related to themselves, to each other, and to the world around them.

All the Axial movements had essential ingredients in common. They were acutely conscious of the suffering that seemed an inescapable part of the human condition, and all stressed the need for a more spiritualised religion that was not so heavily dependent upon external rituals and practice. They had a new concern about the individual conscience and morality. Henceforth it would not be sufficient to perform the conventional rites meticulously; worshippers must also treat their fellow-creatures with respect. All the sages recoiled from the violence of their time, and preached an ethic of compassion and justice. They taught their disciples to look within themselves for truth and not to rely on the teachings of priests and other religious experts. Nothing should be taken on trust, everything should be questioned, and old values, hitherto taken for granted, must be subjected to critical scrutiny. One of the areas that required re-evaluation was, of course, mythology.

When they contemplated the ancient myths, each of the Axial movements adopted a slightly different position. Some were hostile to certain mythical trends; others adopted a *laissez-faire* attitude. All gave their myths a more interior and ethical interpretation. The advent of urban life had meant that mythology was no longer taken for granted. People continued to examine it critically, but when they confronted the mystery of the psyche, they found that they still instinctively turned to the old myths. The stories might have to be recast, but they were still felt to be necessary. If a myth was banished by the more exacting reformers, it sometimes crept back later into the system in a slightly different guise. Even in these more sophisticated religious systems, people found that they could not do without mythology.

But people no longer experienced the sacred as easily as their ancestors. The gods had already begun to retreat from the consciousness of some of the early city-dwellers. People in the Axial countries still yearned for transcendence, but the sacred now seemed remote, and even alien. A gulf now separated mortals from their gods. They no longer shared the same nature; it was no longer possible to believe that gods and men derived from the same divine substance. The early Hebrew myths had imagined a god who could eat and converse with Abraham as a friend[69] but, when the prophets of the Axial Age encountered this same god, he was experienced as a fearful shock, which either endangered their lives, or left them feeling stunned and violated.[70] The supreme reality now seemed impossibly difficult of access. In India, Buddhists felt that they could enter the sacred peace of Nirvana only by mounting a formidable attack on their normal consciousness by means of yoga exercises that were beyond the reach of ordinary folk, while the Jains practised such severe asceticism that some even starved themselves to death. In China, Confucius believed that the Dao, the supreme reality, was now so alien from the world of men that it was better not to speak about it.[71] This radically different religious experience meant that mythology could no longer easily speak about the divine in the old anthropomorphic way.

China has not figured much in our discussion, because in their high culture the Chinese did not tell stories about the gods. There were no tales of divine combat, dying gods or sacred marriages; there were no official pantheons, no cosmogony, and no anthropomorphic gods. The cities had no patron deities, and no urban cult. This does not mean that Chinese society had no mythical underpinning, however. Ancestor worship was of crucial importance, and pointed to a world that had predated the world of human beings. Rituals to departed kinsfolk provided the Chinese with a model for an idealised social order, which was conceived as a family, and governed by the principles of decorum. Rivers, stars, winds and crops all had indwelling spirits which lived harmoniously together in obedience to the Sky God, Di (later also known as Tian: 'heaven'). Unlike other Sky Gods, the Chinese High God did not fade away. He became more prominent at the time of the Shang dynasty (*c.* 1600–mid-eleventh century BCE). The king's legitimacy derived from the fact that he alone had access to Di/Tian, and, according to the principles of the perennial philosophy, he was the earthly counterpart of God – a myth that survived in Chinese culture until the revolution of 1911. Earthly government was identical to the arrangements of heaven; the king's ministers aided him just as Tian was assisted in the governance of the cosmos by the gods of the elements.

The Chinese seemed to have been groping towards

the Axial ethos earlier than the other cultures. In
1126 BCE, a people from the Wei River valley, in the
present-day Shensi province, overthrew the Shang
state and established the Zhou dynasty. The Zhou
claimed that the last Shang king had been corrupt
and that, in his concern for the people's suffering,
Tian had passed his mandate to the Zhou – a myth
that endowed Tian with an ethical character. The
Zhou celebrated the order of heaven in elaborate
ritual ceremonies, accompanied by powerfully
beautiful music. This liturgy was experienced as
an epiphany of a social harmony that was itself
divine. All participants, living and dead, had to
conform to these ceremonies. All beings – spirits,
ancestors and humans – had their special place;
everybody had to subordinate their likes, dislikes
and personal inclinations to the rites, which made
the ideal order of the universe a reality in the
flawed world of men and women. It was the rites
and not the actors who were important; individuals
felt caught up and subsumed into the Sacred World,
which was the foundation of both the cosmos and
their own polity.

By the time of Confucius, however, the Zhou dynasty had fallen into decline and the old order was in ruins. Confucius attributed this anarchy to the neglect of the rituals and the accepted codes of behaviour (*li*) that had taught people how they should comport themselves to one another. Now decorum had been cast aside and people pursued only their own selfish interests. Some of the old myths had pointed out that creativity was based upon self-sacrifice, but the Axial Sages made the ethical consequences of this insight more explicit. This self-immolation had to be practised in daily life by everyone who wished to perfect his humanity.[72] Confucius infused the old Chinese ethos with the Axial virtue of compassion. He promoted the ideal of *ren* ('humaneness'), which required people to 'love others'.[73] He was the first to promulgate the Golden Rule: 'Do not do unto others as you would not have done unto you.'[74] The Axial spirit demanded inner reflection and self-scrutiny, a deliberate analysis of the deeper recesses of the self. You could not behave rightly to others unless you had first examined your own needs, motivation and inclinations; proper respect for others required a process of *shu* ('likening to oneself').[75]

But Confucius realised that this could not be done by an act of will or by rational reflection alone. Absolute transcendence of selfishness could only be achieved through the alchemy of ritual and music, which, like all great art, transfigures human beings at a level that is deeper than the cerebral.[76] Yet it was not enough simply to attend the rituals: it was essential to understand the spirit behind them, which inculcated an attitude of 'yielding' (*rang*) to others in order to overcome pride, resentment and envy.[77] As the worshippers bowed to the other participants, submitted to the demands of the rite, and allowed others to take the lead when required – all to the accompaniment of sublime music – they learned how to behave to their fellows in ordinary transactions and relationships. Confucius looked back to exemplary models of the past. The Chinese had no stories about the gods, but they did revere culture heroes, who were in fact mythical figures but were thought to be historical. Confucius's special heroes were two of the five Sage Kings of remote antiquity. The first was Yao, who had not only taught the Chinese the proper use of ritual and music, but had demonstrated the virtue of *rang*. Because he deemed none of his sons worthy to rule, he chose the virtuous peasant Shun as his successor. Shun had also displayed exceptional selflessness when he had continued to love his father and brothers and treat them with reverence and respect, even though they had tried to kill him.

But for Confucius, ritual, if properly understood, was more important than these mythical stories. There had been a similar development in Vedic India, where the rituals of sacrifice had eclipsed the gods to whom they were offered. The gods gradually retreated from the religious consciousness, and the ritual reformers of the eighth century BCE devised a new liturgy that put the solitary individual at centre-stage. Henceforth men could not rely on the gods for help; they had to create an ordered world for themselves in the ritual arena. The power engendered by these ceremonies, which was known as *Brahman*, was experienced as so overwhelming that it was thought to be the ultimate reality that lay beyond the gods and kept the world in being. Even today, a religious festival can produce the rapture that Indians call *anya manas*, the 'other mind' that is quite different from normal, profane consciousness. The Indian and Chinese emphasis on liturgy reminds us yet again that myth cannot be viewed in isolation from this context. Myth and cultic practice are equal partners, both help to convey a sense of the sacred, and usually do so together, but sometimes ritual takes first place.

The Axial Sages all insisted on a third compo-nent, however. To understand the true meaning of the myth, you must not only perform the rites which give it emotional resonance, but you must also behave in the correct ethical manner. Unless your daily life was informed by what Confucius called *ren, rang* and *shu*, a myth like that of Yao or Shun would remain abstract and opaque. In Vedic India, ritual actions had been called *karma* ('deeds'). The Buddha, however, had no interest in sacrificial ritual. He rede-fined *karma* as the intentions that inspired our ordin-ary actions.[78] Our motives were internal *karma*, mental actions that were far more important than ritual observance, and just as important as external actions. This was a revolution typical of the Axial period, which deepened and interiorised the under-standing of both morality and mythology. Myth had always demanded action. The Axial sages showed that myth would not reveal its full significance, unless it led to the exercise of practical compassion and justice in daily life.

The third-century BCE author of the *Dao De Jing*, traditionally known as Laozi, also had a negative view of traditional ritual. Instead of *li*, he relied on exercises of concentration similar to the Indian practice of yoga. Civilisation, he was convinced, had been a mistake, which had diverted human beings from the true Way (*Dao*). Laozi looked back to a Golden Age of agrarian simplicity, when people lived in small villages with no technology, no art or culture, and no war.[79] This Golden Age, the Chinese believed, had come to an end with the death of the culture hero Shen Nong, who, at immense cost to himself, had taught human beings the science of agriculture. Shen Nong had personally tasted all plants to find out which were edible, and had once been poisoned seventy times in one day. By the third century BCE, when the more powerful kingdoms were swallowing up small states and communities in one destructive war after another, the myth of Shen Nong had changed. He was now regarded as the ideal ruler. It was said that he had governed a decentralised empire, had ploughed his own fields alongside his subjects, and had ruled without ministers, laws or punishments. Idealistic hermits had dropped out of public life to recreate the Shen Nong ideal, and the *Dao De Jing*, which is addressed to the ruler of a small state, gives similar advice. It is best to retreat, lie low and do nothing until the great powers have overreached themselves.

But like all Axial teachers, Laozi was not simply concerned with the practicalities of survival, but with finding a source of transcendent peace in the midst of earthly turbulence. He aspires to the ultimate reality, the Dao, which goes beyond the gods, and is the ineffable basis of all existence. It transcends everything we can conceptualise, and yet if we cultivate an inner emptiness, without selfish desire and without greed, and live in a compassionate manner, we will be in harmony with the Dao and thus transformed. When we give up the goal-directed ethos of civilisation, we will be in tune with the Way things ought to be.[80] Yet just as Laozi appeals to the mythical Golden Age of Shen Nong when describing the ideal polity, he also appeals to traditional myths (which may have been current in popular culture) in order to evoke the Dao. The Dao is the Source of Life, the Perfect Ancestor, and also the Mother. Prehistoric human beings had seen the Great Mother as fierce and violent, but in the new Axial spirit, Laozi gives her the attributes of compassion. She is associated with the selflessness that is inseparable from true creativity.[81] Prehistoric men and women had sometimes enacted a return to the womb by burrowing through subterranean tunnels. Laozi imagines the Sage, the perfected human being, making this return by conforming to the Way of the universe.

Both Laozi and the Buddha were willing to use old myths to help people to understand the new ideas. Believing that animal sacrifice was not only useless but also cruel, the Buddha attacked Vedic ritualism, but was tolerant of traditional mythology. He no longer believed that the gods were efficacious, but he was able to set them quietly to one side, and felt no need to mount an ideological offensive against

them. He also gave the gods a new, symbolic significance. In some of the stories about his life, gods such
as Brahma, the supreme deity, or Mara, lord of death,
seem to be reflections of his own inner states, or
personifications of conflicting mental forces.[82]

But the prophets of Israel could not take this
relaxed attitude. They felt compelled to fight hard
against old myths that they found incompatible with
their Axial reform. For centuries, Israelites had
enjoyed the ritual and mythical life of the Near East,
worshipping Asherah, Baal and Ishtar alongside their
own god, Yahweh. But now that Yahweh seemed so
distant, prophets such as Hosea, Jeremiah and Ezekiel
undertook a radical revision of the old anthropomorphic myths. Because the old stories now seemed
empty, they declared them to be false. Their god
Yahweh, whose towering transcendence showed the
triviality of these old tales, was the *only* god. They
mounted a polemic against the old religion. Yahweh
himself is depicted as having to make a belligerent
bid for the leadership of the Divine Council, point-
ing out that his fellow-gods are neglecting the Axial
virtues of justice and compassion, and will, therefore,

be phased out, dying like mortal men.[83] Culture heroes, such as Joshua, David and King Josiah are shown violently suppressing the local pagan cults,[84] and the effigies of Baal or Marduk are ridiculed as man-made, consisting entirely of gold and silver, and knocked together by a craftsman in a couple of hours.[85]

This was, of course, a reductive view of Middle Eastern paganism. But the history of religion shows that, once a myth ceases to give people intimations of transcendence, it becomes abhorrent. Monotheism, the belief in only one god, was initially a struggle. Many of the Israelites still felt the allure of the old myths, and had to fight this attraction. They felt that they were being torn painfully from the mythical world of their neighbours, and were becoming outsiders. We sense this strain in the distress of Jeremiah, who experienced his god as a pain that convulsed his every limb, or in the strange career of Ezekiel, whose life became an icon of radical discontinuity. Ezekiel is commanded by God to eat excrement; he is forbidden to mourn his dead wife; he is overcome with fearful, uncontrollable trembling.

The Axial prophets felt that they were taking their people into an unknown world, where nothing could be taken for granted, and normal responses were denied.

But eventually this distress gave way to serene confidence, and the religion that we now call Judaism came into being.

Ironically, this new self-assurance came after a great catastrophe. In 586 the Babylonian King Nebuchadrezzar conquered the city of Jerusalem and destroyed the temple of Yahweh. Many of the Israelites were deported to Babylonia, where the exiles were exposed to the towering ziggurats, the rich liturgical life of the city, and the massive temple of Esagila. Yet it was here that paganism lost its attraction. We see the new spirit in the first chapter of Genesis, probably written by a member of the so-called Priestly School, which can be read as a poised, calm polemic against the old belligerent cosmogonies. In calm, ordered prose, this new creation myth looks coolly askance at the Babylonian cosmology. Unlike Marduk, Israel's god does not have to fight desperate battles to create the world; he brings all things into existence effortlessly, by a simple command. The sun, moon, stars, sky and earth are not gods in their own right, hostile to Yahweh. They are subservient to him, and created for a purely practical end. The sea-monster is no Tiamat, but is God's creature and does his bidding. Yahweh's creative act is so superior to Marduk's that it never has to be repeated or renewed. Where the Babylonian gods were engaged in an ongoing battle against the forces of chaos, and needed the rituals of the New Year festival to restore their energies, Yahweh can simply rest on the seventh day, his work complete.

But the Israelites were quite happy to use the old Middle Eastern mythology when it suited them. In the book of Exodus, the crossing of the Sea of Reeds is described precisely as a myth.[86] Immersion in water was traditionally used as a rite of passage; other gods had split a sea in half when they created the world – though what is being brought into being in the Exodus myth is not a cosmos but a people. The prophet we call Second Isaiah, who was active in Babylon in the middle of the sixth century, articulates a clear, unequivocal monotheism. There is no stridency; he has no doubt that Yahweh is the only god; the antagonism has gone. Yet he evokes the ancient creation myths that depict Yahweh fighting sea-monsters to bring the world into being, just like any other Middle Eastern deity, equating this victory over the primal Sea with Yahweh's parting of the Sea of Reeds at the time of the Exodus. Israelites can now expect a similar show of divine strength in their own time, since God is about to reverse the exile and bring them home. The Babylonian author of *The Epic of Gilgamesh* brought ancient history and mythology together, but Second Isaiah goes further. He links the primordial actions of his god with current events.[87]

In Greece, the Axial Age was fuelled by *logos* (reason), which operated at a different level of the mind from myth. Where myth requires either emotional participation or some kind of ritual *mimesis* to make any sense at all, *logos* tries to establish the truth by means of careful inquiry in a way that appeals only to the critical intelligence. In the Greek colonies of Ionia, in what is now Turkey, the first physicists tried to find a rational basis for the old cosmological myths. But this scientific enterprise was still couched in the old mythical and archetypal framework. In a way that was reminiscent of the *Enuma Elish*, they saw the world evolving from some primordial stuff, not because of a divine initiative, but according to the regular laws of the cosmos. For Anaximander (*c.* 611–547), the original *arche* (principle) was quite unlike anything in our human experience. He called it the Infinite; the familiar elements of our world emerged from it in a process governed by alternating heat and cold. Anaximenes (d. *c.* 500) believed that the *arche* was infinite air; while for Heraclitus (fl. *c.* 500) it was fire. These early speculations were as fictional as the old myths, because there was no way they could be verified. The poet Xenophanes (fl. 540–500) realised this and reflected upon the limitations of human thought. He tried to write a rational theology, dismissing the anthropomorphic myths about the gods, and positing a deity who conformed to the science of the *phusikoi*: an abstract, impersonal force, moral but motionless, all-knowing and all-powerful.

Very few people were interested in Ionian physics, the first manifestation of the Axial spirit in Greece.

Before the passion for philosophy took strong root in the fourth century, the Athenians had developed a new type of ritual, the *mimesis* of tragedy, which solemnly reenacted the ancient myths in the context of a religious festival, but at the same time subjected them to close scrutiny. Aeschylus (*c.* 525–456), Sophocles (*c.* 496–405) and Euripedes (480–406) all put the gods on trial, with the audience as the judging tribunal. Myth does not question itself; it demands a degree of self-identification. Tragedy, however, put some distance between itself and the traditional mythology, and queried some of the most fundamental Greek values. Were the gods really fair and just? What was the value of heroism, of Greekness, or democracy? Tragedy came to the fore in a time of transition, a period when the old myths were beginning to lose touch with the new political realities of the city-states. A hero such as Oedipus is still committed to traditional mythical ideals, but they do not help him to solve his dilemma. Where the mythical hero could fight his way through to victory or, at least, to some degree of resolution, there are no such solutions for the tragic hero.

Enmeshed in pain and perplexity, the hero must make conscious choices and accept their consequences.

Yet for all its iconoclasm, tragedy was cast in traditional ritual form. Like any religious rite, it represented a movement from isolated sorrow to communal sharing, but for the first time the inner life was involved in the religious life of the *polis*. The dramas were performed during the festival of Dionysos, the god of transformation, and may have played an important role in the initiation of Athenian youths and their attainment of full citizenship. Like any initiation, tragedy forced the audience to face the unspeakable, and to experience extremity. It is close to the ideology of sacrifice, because it leads to *katharsis*, an interior purification resulting from the violent invasion of heart and mind by the emotions of pity and terror. But this new form of sacrifice was imbued with Axial compassion, because the audience learned to feel the pain of another person as though it were their own, thereby enlarging the scope of their sympathy and humanity.

Plato disliked tragedy, because it was too emotional; he believed that it fed the irrational part of the soul, and that humans could only achieve their full potential through *logos*.[88] He compared myths to old wives' tales. Only logical, rational discourse brings true understanding.[89] Plato's theory of the Eternal Ideas can be seen as a philosophical version of the ancient myth of the divine archetypes, of which mundane things are the merest shadow. But, for Plato, the Ideas of Love, Beauty, Justice and the Good cannot be intuited or apprehended through the insights of myth or ritual, but only through the reasoning powers of the mind. Aristotle was in agreement with Plato. He found the old myths incomprehensible: 'For they make the first principles gods or generated from gods, and they say that whatever did not taste of the nectar and ambrosia became mortal . . . but as regards the actual application of these causes, their statements are beyond our comprehension.' Aristotle was reading myth as though it were a philosophical text. From a scientific perspective, these myths are nonsense, and a serious seeker after truth should 'turn rather to those who reason by means of demonstration'.[90] It seemed that the study of philosophy had caused a rift between *mythos* and *logos*, which had hitherto been complementary.

Yet this was not the whole story. For all his impatience with myth, Plato allowed it an important role in the exploration of ideas that lie *beyond* the scope of philosophical language. We cannot speak of the Good in terms of *logos*, because it is not *a* being but the source of both Being and Knowledge. There are other matters, such as the origin of the cosmos or the birth of the gods, that seem subject to blind causality and so contaminated by the irrational that they cannot be expressed in coherent arguments. So when the subject matter falls *below* philosophical discourse, we must be content with a plausible fable.[91] When he writes of the soul, for example, Plato falls back on the old oriental myth of reincarnation.[92] Aristotle agrees that, while some of the myths about the gods are clearly absurd, the basis of this tradition – 'that all the first substances were gods' – is 'truly divine'.[93]

There was, therefore, a contradiction in Western thought. Greek *logos* seemed to oppose mythology, but philosophers continued to use myth, either seeing it as the primitive forerunner of rational thought or regarding it as indispensable to religious discourse. And indeed, despite the monumental achievements of Greek rationalism during the Axial Age, it had no effect on Greek religion. Greeks continued to sacrifice to the gods, take part in the Eleusinian mysteries, and celebrate their festivals until the sixth century of the Common Era, when this pagan religion was forcibly suppressed by the Emperor Justinian, and replaced by the *mythos* of Christianity.

The Post-Axial Period
(*c.* 200 BCE to *c.* 1500 CE)

Hitherto in our historical survey, we have concentrated on the major intellectual, spiritual and social revolutions that forced human beings to revise their mythology. After the Axial Age, there would be no comparable period of change for over a millennium. In spiritual and religious matters, we still rely on the insights of the Axial sages and philosophers, and the status of myth remained basically the same until the sixteenth century CE. In the rest of this history, we shall concentrate on the West, not just because the next period of innovation began there, but also because Western people had already begun to find mythology problematic. We shall also concentrate on the Western religions, because the three monotheistic faiths claim, at least in part, to be historically rather than mythically based. The other major traditions have a less ambivalent attitude to myth. In

Hinduism, history is regarded as ephemeral and illu-
sory, and therefore unworthy of spiritual consideration. Hindus feel more at home in the archetypal
world of myth. Buddhism is a deeply psychological
religion, and finds mythology, an early form of
psychology, quite congenial. In Confucianism, ritual
has always been more important than mythical narratives. But Jews, Christians and Muslims believe that
their god is active in history and can be experienced
in actual events in this world. Did these events really
happen or are they 'only' myths? Because of the
uneasy attitude to myth which had entered the
Western mind with Plato and Aristotle, monotheists
would periodically try to make their religion conform
to the rational standards of philosophy, but most
would finally conclude that this had been a mistake.

Judaism had a paradoxical attitude towards the
mythology of other peoples. It seemed antagonistic
towards the myths of other nations, but yet would
sometimes draw upon these foreign stories to express
the Jewish vision. Furthermore, Judaism continued
to inspire more myths. One of these was Christianity.
Jesus and his first disciples were Jewish and strongly

rooted in Jewish spirituality, as was St Paul, who can be said to have transformed Jesus into a mythical figure. This is not intended to be pejorative. Jesus was a real historical human being, who was executed in about 30 CE by the Romans, and his first disciples certainly thought that he had – in some sense – risen from the dead. But unless a historical event is mythologised, it cannot become a source of religious inspiration. A myth, it will be recalled, is an event that – in some sense – happened once, but which also happens all the time. An occurrence needs to be liberated, as it were, from the confines of a specific period and brought into the lives of contemporary worshippers, or it will remain a unique, unrepeatable incident, or even a historical freak that cannot really touch the lives of others. We do not know what actually happened when the people of Israel escaped from Egypt and crossed the Sea of Reeds, because the story has been written as a myth. The rituals of Passover have for centuries made this tale central to the spiritual lives of Jews, who are told that each one of them must consider himself to be of the generation that escaped from Egypt. A myth cannot be correctly understood without a transformative ritual, which brings it into the lives and hearts of generations of worshippers. A myth demands action: the myth of the Exodus demands that Jews cultivate an appreciation of freedom as a sacred value, and refuse either to be enslaved themselves or to oppress others. By ritual practice and ethical response, the story has ceased to be an event in the distant past, and has become a living reality.

St Paul did the same with Jesus. He was not much interested in Jesus's teachings, which he rarely quotes, or in the events of his earthly life. 'Even if we did once know Christ in the flesh,' he wrote to his Corinthian converts, 'that is not how we know him now.'[94] What was important was the 'mystery' (a word which has the same etymological root as the Greek *mythos*) of his death and resurrection. Paul had transformed Jesus into the timeless, mythical hero who dies and is raised to new life. After his crucifixion, Jesus had been exalted by God to a uniquely high status, had achieved an 'ascent' to a higher mode of being.[95] But everybody who went through the initiation of baptism (the traditional transformation by immersion) entered into Jesus's death and would share his new life.[96] Jesus was no longer a mere historical figure but a spiritual reality in the lives of Christians by means of ritual and the ethical discipline of living the same selfless life as Jesus himself.[97] Christians no longer knew him 'in the flesh' but they would encounter him in other human beings, in the study of scripture, and in the Eucharist.[98] They knew that this myth was true, not because of the historical evidence, but because they *had* experienced transformation. Thus the death and 'raising up' of Jesus was a myth: it had happened once to Jesus, and was now happening all the time.

Christianity was one latter-day restatement of Axial Age monotheism; the other was Islam. Muslims regard the Prophet Muhammad (*c.* 570–632 CE) as the successor of the biblical prophets and of Jesus. The Koran, the scripture that he brought to the Arabs, had no problem with myth. Every single one of its verses is called an *ayah*, a parable. All the stories about the prophets – Adam, Noah, Abraham, Moses or Jesus – are *ayat*, 'parables, similitudes', because we can only speak about the divine in terms of signs and symbols. The Arabic word *qur'an* means 'recitation'. The scripture is not to be perused privately for information, like a secular manual, but recited in the sacred context of the mosque, and it will not reveal its full significance unless a Muslim lives according to its ethical precepts.

Because of the mythical dimension of these historical religions, Jews, Christians and Muslims continued to use mythology to explain their insights or to respond to a crisis. Their mystics all had recourse to myth. The words mysticism and mystery are both related to a Greek verb meaning: 'to close the eyes or the mouth'. Both refer to experiences that are obscure and ineffable, because they are beyond speech, and relate to the inner rather than the external world. Mystics make a journey into the depths of the psyche by means of the disciplines of concentration that have been developed in all the religious traditions and have become a version of the hero's mythical quest. Because mythology charts this hidden, interior dimension, it is natural for mystics to describe their experiences in myths that might, at first glance, seem inimical to the orthodoxy of their tradition.

This is especially clear in the Kabbalah, the Jewish mystical tradition. We have seen that the biblical writers were hostile to Babylonian or Syrian mythology. But Kabbalists imagined a process of divine evolution that is not dissimilar to the gradualist theogony described in the *Enuma Elish*. From the inscrutable and unknowable godhead, which mystics called En 'Sof' ('Without End'), ten divine *sefirot* ('numerations') emerged, ten emanations that represent the process whereby En 'Sof' descended from Its lonely solitude and made Itself known to human beings.[99] Each *sefirah* is a stage in this unfolding revelation, and has its own symbolic name. Each makes the mystery of the godhead more accessible to the limited human mind. Each is a Word of God, and also the means by which God created the world. The last *sefirah* was called the Shekhinah, the divine presence of God on earth. The Shekhinah was often imagined as a woman, as the female aspect of God. Some Kabbalists even imagined the male and female elements of the divinity engaged in sexual congress, an image of wholeness and reintegration. In some forms of Kabbalah, the Shekhinah wanders through the world, a bride who is lost and alienated from the godhead, in exile from the divine realm, and yearning to return to her source. By careful observance of the Law of Moses, Kabbalists can end the exile of the Shekhinah and restore the world to God. In biblical times, Jews hated the local cult of such goddesses as Anat, who had wandered through the world in search of her divine spouse and celebrated her sexual reunion with Baal. But when Jews tried to find a way to express their mystical apprehension of the divine, this reviled, pagan myth was given tacit Jewish endorsement.

Kabbalah seemed to have no biblical warrant, but before the modern period it was generally taken for granted that there was no 'official' version of a myth. People had always felt free to develop a new myth or a radical interpretation of an old mythical narrative. Kabbalists did not read the Bible in a literal way; they developed an exegesis that made every single word of the biblical text refer to one or other of the *sefirot*. Each verse of, for example, the first chapter of Genesis described an event that had its counterpart in the hidden life of God. Kabbalists even felt free to devise a new creation myth that bore no resemblance to the Genesis account. After the Jews were deported from Spain by the Catholic monarchs Ferdinand and Isabella in 1492, many could no longer relate to the calm orderly creation myth in Genesis I, so the Kabbalist Isaac Luria (1534–72) told an entirely different creation story, full of false starts, divine mistakes, explosions, violent reversals and disasters, which resulted in a flawed creation, where everything was in the wrong place. Far from shocking the Jewish people by its unorthodox departure from the biblical story, Lurianic Kabbalah became a Jewish mass-movement. It reflected the tragic experience of sixteenth-century Jews, but the myth did not stand alone. Luria devised special rituals, methods of meditation and ethical disciplines that gave life to the myth and made it a spiritual reality in the lives of Jews all over the world.

There are similar examples in Christian and Muslim history. When the Roman Empire fell in the West, St Augustine (354–430), bishop of Hippo in North Africa, reinterpreted the myth of Adam and Eve and developed the myth of Original Sin. Because of Adam's disobedience, God had condemned the entire human race to eternal damnation (another idea that has no biblical foundation). The inherited guilt was passed on to all Adam's descendants through the sexual act, which was polluted by 'concupiscence', the irrational desire to take pleasure in mere creatures rather than in God, a permanent effect of the first sin. Concupiscence was most fully evident in the sexual act, when God is quite forgotten and creatures revel shamelessly in one another. This vision of reason dragged down by a chaos of sensations and lawless passion was disturbingly similar to the spectacle of Rome, source of rationality, law and order in the West, brought low by the barbarian tribes. Western Christians often regard the myth of Original Sin as essential to their faith, but the Greek Orthodox of Byzantium, where Rome did not fall, have never fully endorsed this doctrine, do not believe that Jesus died to save us from the effects of the Original Sin, and have asserted that God would have become human even if Adam had not sinned.

In Islam, mystics also evolved myths of separation and return to God. It was said that the Prophet

Muhammad had made a mystical ascent to the Throne of God from the Temple Mount in Jerusalem. This myth has become the archetype of Muslim spirituality, and the Sufis use this mythical journey to symbolise the Prophet's perfect act of *islam* or 'surrender' to God. Shii Muslims developed a mythical view of the Prophet's male descendants, who were their *imams* ('leaders'). Each Imam was an incarnation of the divine *ilm* ('knowledge'). When the line died out, they said that the last Imam had gone into a state of 'occultation', and that one day he would return to inaugurate an era of justice and peace. At this point, Shiism was primarily a mystical movement and, without special disciplines of meditation and spiritual exegesis, this myth made no sense. Shiis certainly did not intend their myths to be interpreted literally. The myth of the Imamate, which might seem to flout Muslim orthodoxy, was a symbolic way of expressing the mystics' sense of a sacred presence, immanent and accessible in a turbulent and dangerous world. The Hidden Imam had become a myth; by his removal from normal history, he had been liberated from the confines of space and time, and, paradoxically, had become a more vivid presence in the lives of Shiis than when he had lived under house arrest, by order of the Abbasid Caliph. The story expresses our sense of the sacred as elusive and tantalisingly absent, in the world but not of it.

But because of the division between *mythos* and *logos* experienced by the Greeks, some Jews, Christians and Muslims became uneasy about the rich mythical vein in their traditions. When Plato and Aristotle were translated into Arabic during the eighth and ninth centuries, some Muslims tried to make the religion of the Koran a religion of *logos*. They evolved 'proofs' for the existence of Allah, modelled on Aristotle's demonstration of the First Cause. These Faylasufs, as they were called, wanted to purge Islam of what they regarded as primitive, mythical elements. They had a difficult task, since the god of the philosophers took no notice of mundane events, did not reveal himself in history, had not created the world, and did not even know that human beings existed. Nevertheless the Faylasufs did some interesting work, together with the Jews in the Islamic empire who set about the task of rationalising the religion of the Bible. Nevertheless, Falsafah remained a minority pursuit, confined to a small intellectual elite. The First Cause might be more logical than the god of the Bible and the Koran, but it is hard for most people to work up any interest in a deity who is so uninterested in them.

Significantly, the Greek Orthodox Christians despised this rational project. They knew their own Hellenic tradition and knew only too well that *logos* and *mythos* could not, as Plato had explained, prove the existence of the Good. In their view, the study of theology could not be a rational exercise. Using reason to discuss the sacred was about as pointless as trying to eat soup with a fork. Theology was only valid if pursued together with prayer and liturgy. Muslims and Jews eventually reached the same conclusion. By the eleventh century, Muslims had decided that philosophy must be wedded with spirituality, ritual and prayer, and the mythical, mystical religion of the Sufis became the normative form of Islam until the end of the nineteenth century. Similarly, Jews discovered that when they were afflicted by such tragedies as their expulsion from

Spain, the rational religion of their philosophers could not help them, and they turned instead to the myths of the Kabbalah, which reached through the cerebral level of the mind and touched the inner source of their anguish and yearning. They had all returned to the old view of the complementarity of mythology and reason. *Logos* was indispensable in the realm of medicine, mathematics and natural science — in which Muslims in particular excelled. But when they wanted to find ultimate meaning and significance in their lives, when they sought to alleviate their despair, or wished to explore the inner regions of their personality, they had entered the domain of myth.

But in the eleventh and twelfth centuries, Christians in Western Europe rediscovered the works of Plato and Aristotle that had been lost to them during the Dark Age that had followed the collapse of the Roman Empire. Just at the moment when Jews and Muslims were beginning to retreat from the attempt to rationalise their mythology, Western Christians seized on the project with an enthusiasm that they would never entirely lose. They had started to lose touch with the meaning of myth. Perhaps it was not surprising, therefore, that the next great transformation in human history, which would make it very difficult for people to think mythically, had its origins in Western Europe.

The Great Western Transformation
(*c.* 1500 to 2000)

During the sixteenth century, almost by trial and error, the people of Europe and, later, in what would become the United States of America, had begun to create a civilisation that was without precedent in world history, and during the nineteenth and twentieth centuries it would spread to other parts of the globe. This was the last of the great revolutions in human experience. Like the discovery of agriculture or the invention of the city, it would have a profound impact, whose effect we are only now beginning to appreciate. Life would never be the same again, and perhaps the most significant – and potentially disastrous – result of this new experiment was the death of mythology.

Western modernity was the child of *logos*. It was founded on a different economic basis. Instead of relying on a surplus of agricultural produce, like all pre-modern civilisations, the new Western societies were founded on the technological replication of resources and the constant reinvestment of capital. This freed modern society from many of the constraints of traditional cultures, whose agrarian base had inevitably been precarious. Hitherto an invention or an idea that required too much capital outlay was likely to be shelved, because no society before our own could afford the ceaseless replication of the infrastructure that we now take for granted. Agrarian societies were vulnerable because they depended upon such variables as harvests and soil erosion. An empire would expand and increase its commitments and, inevitably, outrun its financial base. But the West developed an economy that seemed, potentially, to be indefinitely renewable. Instead of looking back to the past and conserving what had been achieved, as had been the habit of the premodern civilisations, Western people began to look forward. The long process of modernisation, which took Europe some three centuries, involved a series of profound changes: industrialisation, the transformation of agriculture, political and social revolutions to reorganise

society to meet the new conditions, and an intellectual 'enlightenment' that denigrated myth as useless,
false and outmoded.

The Western achievement relied on the triumph
of the pragmatic, scientific spirit. Efficiency was the
new watchword. Everything had to work. A new idea
or an invention had to be capable of rational proof
and be shown to conform to the external world.
Unlike myth, *logos* must correspond to facts; it is
essentially practical; it is the mode of thought we
use when we want to get something done; it
constantly looks ahead to achieve a greater control
over our environment or to discover something fresh.
The new hero of Western society was henceforth the
scientist or the inventor, who was venturing into
uncharted realms for the sake of his society. He would
often have to overthrow old sanctities – just as the
Axial sages had done. But the heroes of Western
modernity would be technological or scientific
geniuses of *logos*, not the spiritual geniuses inspired
by *mythos*. This meant that intuitive, mythical modes
of thought would be neglected in favour of the more
pragmatic, logical spirit of scientific rationality.

Because most Western people did not use myth, many would lose all sense of what it was.

There was a new optimism in the West. People felt that they had more control over their environment. There were no more sacred, unalterable laws. Thanks to their scientific discoveries, they could manipulate nature and improve their lot. The discoveries of modern medicine, hygiene, labour-saving technologies and improved methods of transport revolutionised the lives of Western people for the better. But *logos* had never been able to provide human beings with the sense of significance that they seemed to require. It had been myth that had given structure and meaning to life, but as modernisation progressed and *logos* achieved such spectacular results, mythology was increasingly discredited. As early as the sixteenth century, we see more evidence of a numbing despair, a creeping mental paralysis, and a sense of impotence and rage as the old mythical way of thought crumbled and nothing new appeared to take its place. We are seeing a similar anomie today in developing countries that are still in the earlier stages of modernisation.

In the sixteenth century, this alienation was apparent in the reformers who tried to make European religion more streamlined, efficient and modern. Martin Luther (1483–1546) was prey to agonising depressions and paroxysms of rage. Ulrich Zwingli (1484–1531) and John Calvin (1509–64) both shared Luther's utter helplessness before the trials of human existence – a dis-ease that impelled them to find a solution. Their reformed Christianity showed how antagonistic the dawning modern spirit was to the mythical consciousness. In premodern religion, likeness had been experienced as identity, so that a symbol was one with the reality it represented. Now, according to the reformers, a rite such as the Eucharist was 'only' a symbol – something essentially separate. Like any premodern rite, the Mass had reenacted Christ's sacrificial death, which because it was mythical was timeless, and made it a present reality. For the reformers, it was simply a memorial of a bygone event. There was a new emphasis on scripture, but the modern invention of printing and the new widespread literacy altered people's perception of the sacred text. Silent, solitary reading replaced liturgical recitation. People could now know the Bible in greater detail and form their own opinions, but now that it was no longer read in a ritual context, it was easy to approach it in a secular manner for factual information, like any other modern text.

Like most things in life, many of the modern discoveries were also problematic. The new astronomy opened up an enthralling view of the cosmos. Nicolas Copernicus (1473–1543) saw his scientific investigations as a religious activity that filled him with awe. But his findings were disturbing. Myth had made human beings believe that they were bound up with the essence of the universe, yet now it appeared that they had only a peripheral place on an undistinguished planet revolving around a minor star. They could no longer trust their own perceptions, because the earth that seemed static was actually in rapid motion. They were increasingly encouraged to have their own ideas, but they were more and more in thrall to modern 'experts' who alone could decipher the nature of things.

In Britain, Francis Bacon (1561–1626) made a declaration of independence, to emancipate science from the shackles of mythology. In the *Advancement of Learning* (1605), he proclaimed a new and glorious era. Science would put an end to human misery and save the world. Nothing must impede this development. All the myths of religion should be subjected to stringent criticism and if they contradicted the proven facts they must be cast aside. Reason alone gave access to this truth. The first scientist wholly to absorb this empirical ethos was probably Sir Isaac Newton (1642–1727), who synthesised the findings of his predecessors by a rigorous use of the evolving scientific disciplines of experiment and deduction. He believed that he was bringing his fellow human beings unprecedented and certain information about the world, that the cosmic system he had discovered coincided completely with the facts, and that it proved the existence of God, the great 'Mechanick' who had brought the intricate machine of the universe into being.

But this total immersion in *logos* made it impossible for Newton to appreciate the more intuitive forms of perception. For him, mythology and mysticism were primitive modes of thought. He felt that he had a mission to purge Christianity of such doctrines as the Trinity, which defied the laws of logic. He was quite unable to see that this doctrine had been devised by the Greek theologians of the fourth century precisely as a myth, similar to that of the Jewish Kabbalists. As Gregory, Bishop of Nyssa (335–395), had explained, Father, Son and Spirit were not objective, ontological facts but simply 'terms that we use' to express the way in which the 'unnameable and unspeakable' divine nature adapts itself to the limitations of our human minds.[100] You could not prove the existence of the Trinity by rational means. It was no more demonstrable than the elusive meaning of music or poetry. But Newton could only approach the Trinity rationally. If something could not be explained logically, it was false. ''Tis the temper of the hot and superstitious part of mankind in matters of religion,' he wrote irritably, 'ever to be fond of mysteries & for that reason to like best what they understand least.'[101] Today's cosmologists no longer believe in Newton's rational god, but many Western people share his preference for reason and his uneasiness with myth, even in religious matters. Like Newton, they think that God should be an objective, demonstrable reality. Hence a significant number of Western Christians have problems with the Trinity. Like Newton, they fail to understand that the Trinitarian myth was designed to remind Christians that they should not even attempt to think of the divine in terms of a simple personality.[102]

Scientific *logos* and myth were becoming incompatible. Hitherto science had been conducted within a comprehensive mythology that explained its significance. The French mathematician Blaise Pascal (1623–62), a deeply religious man, was filled with horror when he contemplated the 'eternal silence' of the infinite universe opened up by modern science.

When I see the blind and wretched state of men, when I survey the whole universe in its deadness, and man left to himself with no light, as though lost in this corner of the universe without knowing who put him there, what he has to do, or what will become of him when he dies, incapable of knowing anything, I am moved to terror, like a man transported in his sleep

to some terrifying desert island, who wakes up
quite lost, with no means of escape. Then I
marvel that so wretched a state does not drive
people to despair.[103]

This type of alienation has also been part of the
modern experience.

The cloud seemed to lift during the eighteenth-
century Enlightenment. John Locke (1632–1704)
realised that it was impossible to prove the existence
of the sacred, but he had no doubt that God existed
and that humanity had entered a more positive era.
The German and French Enlightenment philosophers
saw the old mystical and mythical religions as
outmoded. So did the British theologians John Toland
(1670–1722) and Matthew Tindal (1655–1733). *Logos*
alone could lead us to truth, and Christianity must
get rid of the mysterious and the mythical. The old
myths were beginning to be interpreted as though
they were *logoi*, an entirely new development which
was doomed to disappoint, because these stories were
not and never had been factual.

Paradoxically, however, the Age of Reason witnessed

an irruption of irrationality. The great Witch Craze of the sixteenth and seventeenth centuries, which raged through many of the Catholic and Protestant countries of Europe, showed that scientific rationalism could not always hold the darker forces of the mind at bay. The Witch Craze was a collective demonic fantasy that led to the execution and torture of thousands of men and women. People believed that witches had sex with devils, and flew through the air to attend satanic orgies. Without a powerful mythology to explain people's unconscious fears, they tried to rationalise those fears into 'fact'. Fearful and destructive un-reason has always been part of the human experience, and it still is. It emerged very strongly in the new Christian movements that attempted to translate the ideals of the Enlightenment into a religious form. Quakers were so-called because they used to tremble, howl and yell during their meetings. The Puritans, many of whom were successful capitalists and good scientists, also had a tumultuous spirituality and traumatic conversion experiences, which many were ill equipped to sustain. A significant number fell into depressive states, and some even committed suicide.[104] The same syndrome can be seen in the First Great Awakening in New England (1734–40). Everybody was attempting to be a mystic and achieve alternative psychic states. But the higher states of mysticism were not for everybody. It required special talent, temperament and one-to-one training. A group experience of untaught, unskilled individuals could lead to mass hysteria and even mental illness.

By the nineteenth century, people in Europe were beginning to think that religion was actually harmful. Ludwig Feuerbach (1804–72) argued that it alienated people from their humanity, and Karl Marx (1818–83) saw religion as the symptom of a sick society. And indeed the mythological religion of the period could create an unhealthy conflict. This was the scientific age, and people wanted to believe that their traditions were in line with the new era, but this was impossible if you thought that these myths should be understood literally. Hence the furore occasioned by *The Origin of Species* (1858), published by Charles Darwin (1809–82). The book was not intended as an attack on religion, but was a sober exploration of a scientific hypothesis. But because by this time people were reading the cosmogonies of Genesis as though they were factual, many Christians felt – and still feel – that the whole edifice of faith was in jeopardy. Creation stories had never been regarded as historically accurate; their purpose was therapeutic. But once you start reading Genesis as scientifically valid, you have bad science and bad religion.

The new Higher Criticism, which applied the modern scientific methodology to the Bible itself, showed that it was impossible to read the Bible literally. Some of its claims were demonstrably untrue. The Pentateuch had not been written by Moses, but much later and by a number of different authors; King David had not composed the Psalms; and most of the miracle stories were literary tropes. The biblical narratives were 'myths' and, in popular parlance, that meant that they were not true. The Higher Criticism is still a bugbear of Protestant Fundamentalists, who claim that every word of the Bible is literally, scientifically and historically true – an untenable position that leads to denial and defensive polemic.

By the end of the nineteenth century, the severance of *logos* and *mythos* seemed complete. Crusaders such as Thomas H. Huxley (1825–95) believed that they had a fight on their hands. People must choose between mythology and rational science, and there could be no compromise. Reason alone was truthful and the myths of religion truthless. But truth had been narrowed down to what was 'demonstrated and demonstrable',[105] which, religion aside, would exclude the truths told by art or music. By treating myth as though it were rational, modern scientists, critics and philosophers had made it incredible. In 1882, Freidrich Nietzsche (1844–1900) proclaimed that God was dead. In a sense, he was right. Without myth, cult, ritual and ethical living, the sense of the sacred dies. By making 'God' a wholly notional truth, reached by the critical intellect alone, modern men and women had killed it for themselves. The Madman in Nietzsche's parable in *The Gay Science* believed that God's death had torn humanity from its roots. 'Is there still an above or below?' he asked. 'Do we not stray, as though through an infinite nothingness?'[106]

Mythical thinking and practice had helped people to face the prospect of extinction and nothingness, and to come through it with a degree of acceptance.

Without this discipline, it has been difficult for many to avoid despair. The twentieth century presented us with one nihilistic icon after another, and many of the extravagant hopes of modernity and the Enlightenment were shown to be false. The sinking of the *Titanic* in 1912 showed the frailty of technology; the First World War revealed that science, our friend, could also be applied with lethal effect to weaponry; Auschwitz, the Gulag and Bosnia spelled out what could happen when all sense of sacredness is lost. We learned that a rational education did not redeem humanity from barbarism, and that a concentration camp could exist in the same vicinity as a great university. The explosion of the first atomic bombs over Hiroshima and Nagasaki laid bare the germ of nihilistic self-destruction at the heart of modern culture; and the attack on the World Trade Center on 11 September 2001 showed that the benefits of modernity – technology, ease of travel and global communications – could be made instruments of terror.

Logos has in many ways transformed our lives for the better, but this has not been an unmitigated triumph. Our demythologised world is very comfortable for many of us who are fortunate enough to live in first-world countries, but it is not the earthly paradise predicted by Bacon and Locke. When we contemplate the dark epiphanies of the twentieth century, we see that modern anxiety is not simply the result of self-indulgent neurosis. We are facing something unprecedented. Other societies saw death as a transition to other modes of being. They did not nurture simplistic and vulgar ideas of an afterlife, but devised rites and myths that helped people to face the unspeakable. In no other culture would anybody settle down in the middle of a rite of passage or an initiation, with the horror unresolved. But this is what we have to do in the absence of a viable mythology. There is a moving and even heroic asceticism in the current rejection of myth. But purely linear, logical and historical modes of thought have debarred many of us from therapies and devices that have enabled men and women to draw on the full resources of their humanity in order to live with the unacceptable.

We may be more sophisticated in material ways, but we have not advanced spiritually beyond the Axial

Age: because of our suppression of *mythos* we may even have regressed. We still long to 'get beyond' our immediate circumstances, and to enter a 'full time', a more intense, fulfilling existence. We try to enter this dimension by means of art, rock music, drugs or by entering the larger-than-life perspective of film. We still seek heroes. Elvis Presley and Princess Diana were both made into instant mythical beings, even objects of religious cult. But there is something unbalanced about this adulation. The myth of the hero was not intended to provide us with icons to admire, but was designed to tap into the vein of heroism within ourselves. Myth must lead to imitation or participation, not passive contemplation. We no longer know how to manage our mythical lives in a way that is spiritually challenging and transformative.

We must disabuse ourselves of the nineteenth-century fallacy that myth is false or that it represents an inferior mode of thought. We cannot completely recreate ourselves, cancel out the rational bias of our education, and return to a pre-modern sensibility. But we can acquire a more educated attitude to mythology. We are myth-making creatures and, during the twentieth century, we saw some very destructive modern myths, which have ended in massacre and genocide. These myths have failed because they do not meet the criteria of the Axial Age. They have not been infused with the spirit of compassion, respect for the sacredness of all life, or with what Confucius called 'leaning'. These destructive mythologies have been narrowly racial, ethnic, denominational and egotistic, an attempt to exalt the self by demonising the other. Any such myth has failed modernity, which has created a global village in which all human beings now find themselves in the same predicament. We cannot counter these bad myths with reason alone, because undiluted *logos* cannot deal with such deep-rooted, unexorcised fears, desires and neuroses. That is the role of an ethically and spiritually informed mythology.

We need myths that will help us to identify with all our fellow-beings, not simply with those who belong to our ethnic, national or ideological tribe. We need myths that help us to realise the importance of compassion, which is not always regarded as suffi-ciently productive or efficient in our pragmatic, rational world. We need myths that help us to create a spiritual attitude, to see beyond our immediate requirements, and enable us to experience a transcendent value that challenges our solipsistic selfishness. We need myths that help us to venerate the earth as sacred once again, instead of merely using it as a 'resource'. This is crucial, because unless there is some kind of spiritual revolution that is able to keep abreast of our technological genius, we will not save our planet.

In 1922, T.S. Eliot depicted the spiritual disintegration of Western culture in his landmark poem *The Waste Land*. In the myth of the Holy Grail, the wasteland is a place where people live inauthentic lives, blindly following the norms of their society without the conviction that comes from deeper understanding. How was it possible to put down creative roots in the 'stony rubbish' of modernity where people had lost touch with the mythical underpinning of their culture? Instead of understanding the inner coherence of their tradition, they know 'only a heap of broken images'. By means of poignant, lapidary allusions to the mythology of the past – to European,

Sanskrit, Buddhist, biblical, Greek and Roman myths – Eliot laid bare the sterility of contemporary life: its alienation, ennui, nihilism, superstition, egotism and despair. As he confronts the imminent demise of Western civilisation, his narrator concludes: 'These fragments I have shored against my ruins.' The broken insights of the past that he has gathered together in his poem can save us. When we have pieced them together and recognised their common core, we can reclaim the wasteland in which we live.

Eliot's poem was prophetic. It has been writers and artists, rather than religious leaders, who have stepped into the vacuum and attempted to reacquaint us with the mythological wisdom of the past. In their attempt to find an antidote to the sterility and heartless cruelty of some aspects of modernity, painters, for example, have turned to mythological themes. On 26 April 1937, at the height of the Spanish Civil War, Nazi planes, under the orders of General Franco, attacked the Basque capital of Guernica on its market-day, killing 1654 of its 7000 inhabitants. A few months later, Pablo Picasso exhibited *Guernica* at the International Exhibition in Paris. This modern, secular crucifixion shocked his contemporaries, and yet, like *The Waste Land*, it was a prophetic statement, and also a rallying cry against the inhumanity of our brave new world.

It is a painting that is suffused with compassion, the ability to *feel with* the agony of others. Sacrifice had inspired some of the earliest mythical speculations. In the Palaeolithic period, human beings had felt a disturbing kinship with the animals that they hunted and killed. They expressed their inchoate distress in the rituals of sacrifice, which honoured the beasts which laid down their lives for the sake of humanity. In *Guernica*, humans and animals, both victims of indiscriminate, heedless slaughter, lie together in a mangled heap, the screaming horse inextricably entwined with the decapitated human figure. Recalling the women at the foot of the cross in countless depictions of Jesus's crucifixion, two women gaze at the wounded horse in sorrowful empathy with its pain. In prehistoric society, the Great Mother had been an implacable huntress, but in Picasso's picture, the mother, who holds the limp body of her dead child, has become a victim, uttering a silent scream.

Behind her is a bull, which, Picasso said, represented brutality. Picasso had always been fascinated by the spectacular rituals of the bullfight, Spain's national sport, which had its roots in the sacrificial ceremonial of antiquity. Picasso's bull does not look savage; he stands with the other victims, swishing his tail and surveying the scene. Perhaps, it has been suggested, he has reached that moment in the bullfight when he stands back from the action to consider his next move. But as a sacrificial victim himself, the bull, symbol of brutality, is doomed. So too – Picasso may be suggesting – is modern humanity, which – though Picasso could not have known this – was only just beginning to explore the full potential of its self-destructive and rationally-calculated violence.

Novelists have also turned to mythology to explore the modern dilemma. We need think only of James Joyce's *Ulysses*, published in the same year as *The Waste Land*, in which the experience of Joyce's contemporary protagonists corresponds to episodes in Homer's *Odyssey*. Magical realists – Jorge Luis Borges, Günter Grass, Italo Calvino, Angela Carter and Salman Rushdie – have challenged the hegemony of *logos* by combining the realistic with the inexplicable, and everyday reason with the mythical logic of dream and fairy tale. Other novelists have looked into the future. George Orwell's *Nineteen Eighty-Four* (1949) warns against the dangers of a police state in which might alone is right and the past is constantly modified to fit the present. The precise implications of Orwell's message have been much debated, but, like the great myths of the past, it has entered popular consciousness. Many of its phrases and images, including the title itself, have passed into ordinary speech: Big Brother, Doublethink, Newspeak and Room 101 are still used to identify trends and characteristics of modern life, even by people who have never read the novel.

But can a secular novel really replicate traditional myth, with its gods and goddesses? We have seen that, in the pre-modern world, the divine was rarely regarded in the metaphysical terms imposed upon it by Western *logos*, but was usually used to help people to understand their humanity. As people's circumstances changed, the gods often receded, taking a marginal place in mythology and religion; sometimes they disappeared altogether. There is nothing new in the godless mythologies of contemporary novels, which grapple with many of the same intractable and elusive problems of the human condition as the ancient myths, and make us realise that – whatever the status of the gods – human beings are more than their material circumstances and that all have sacred, numinous value.

Because the novelist and the artist are operating at the same level of consciousness as mythmakers, they naturally resort to the same themes. Joseph Conrad's *Heart of Darkness* can be seen as a heroic quest and initiation that has gone wrong. Published in 1902, just before the West began its great disillusion, the novel describes the sojourn of the ultra-civilised Mr Kurtz deep in the African jungle. In traditional mythology, the hero left the security of the social world behind. Often he had to descend into the depths of the earth, where he would meet an unsuspected aspect of himself. The experience of isolation and deprivation could result in psychological breakdown, which led to vital new insight. If he succeeded, the hero returned to his people with something new and precious. In Conrad's novel, the labyrinthine, sinister African river recalls the subterranean tunnels of Lascaux, through which the initiates crawled back into the womb of the earth. In the underworld of the primeval jungle, Kurtz does indeed look into the darkness of his heart, but remains stuck in his regression and dies spiritually. He becomes a shaman *manqué*, with no respect but only contempt for the African community that he abuses. The mythical hero learned that, if he died to himself, he would be reborn to new life; but Kurtz is caught in the toils of a sterile egotism, and when he finally appears in the novel, he has the obscenity of an animate corpse. Obsessed with his own fame, Kurtz seeks not heroism, but only barren celebrity. He cannot make a heroic affirmation of life: his dying words are 'The horror! The horror!'. T.S. Eliot made Kurtz's last words the epigraph of *The Waste Land*. Conrad, a true prophet, had already looked into the triviality, selfishness, greed, nihilism and despair of the twentieth century.

Thomas Mann also used the motif of initiation in *The Magic Mountain* (1924), which takes place during another tragic juncture in Western history. He confessed that this had not been his original intention, but when a young Harvard scholar pointed out to him that the novel is a modern example of 'The Quester Hero', he immediately realised that this was in fact the case. The mythology of the heroic quest was embedded in his subconscious and he drew upon it without realising what he had done. The Davos sanatorium of Mann's novel was to become 'a shrine of the initiatory rites, a place of adventurous investigation into the mystery of life'. Hans Castorp, his hero, is a searcher for the Holy Grail, symbol of the 'knowledge, wisdom and consecration' that gives meaning to life. Castorp 'voluntarily embraces disease and death, because his very first contact with them gives promise of extraordinary advancement, bound up, of course, with correspondingly great risks'. And yet, at the same time, this modern initiation shares the chronic triviality of the twentieth century. Mann saw the patients in the sanatorium forming a 'charmed circle of isolation and individualism'. Where the traditional seeker wanted to benefit his society, Castorp was engaged in a solipsistic, parasitic and ultimately pointless quest.[107] He spends seven years on his magic mountain, dreaming his grand dream of humanity, only to die in the First World War, which can be described as the collective suicide of Europe.

Malcolm Lowry's *Under the Volcano* (1947) is set in Mexico on the brink of the Second World War. It traces the last day in the life of the Consul, an alcoholic, who is not only the *alter ego* of Lowry himself, but – it is made clear – also Everyman. The book opens in the Cantina del Bosque, which recalls the 'dark wood' of Dante's Inferno, on the Day of the Dead, when the deceased are believed to commune with the living. Throughout the novel, Lowry explores the ancient mythical insight that life and death are inseparable. The novel constantly juxtaposes the teeming life and beauty of the Mexican landscape – a Garden of Eden – with the infernal imagery of death and darkness. Apparently trivial details acquire universal meaning. People shelter from a storm like the war victims who are hiding in air-raid shelters all over the world; the lights of the cinema go out, just as Europe is plunging into darkness. The advertisement for the film *Las Manos de Orlac*, with its bloodstained hands, reminds us of the collective guilt of humanity; a Ferris wheel symbolises the passing of time; a dying peasant by the roadside reminds us that people all over the globe are dying unheeded. As the Consul becomes chronically intoxicated, his surroundings acquire hallucinatory intensity in which incidents and objects transcend their particularity. In ancient mythology, everything had sacred significance and not a single object or activity was profane. As the Day of the Dead proceeds in Lowry's novel, nothing is neutral: everything is loaded with fateful significance.

The novel depicts the drunkenness of the world before 1939. Every drink that the Consul takes brings him one step closer to his inevitable death. Like the Consul, humanity is out of control and lurching towards disaster. Caught up in a death wish, it is losing its capacity for life and clear vision. The Kabbalah compares a mystic who abuses his powers with a drunkard. This image is central to the novel: like a magician who has lost his way, human beings have unleashed powers that they cannot control, which will ultimately destroy their world. Lowry has told us that he was thinking here of the atomic bomb. And yet the novel is not itself nihilistic, there is deep compassion in its evocation of the pathos, beauty and loveable absurdity of humanity.

We have seen that a myth could never be approached in a purely profane setting. It was only comprehensible in a liturgical context that set it apart from everyday life; it must be experienced as part of a process of personal transformation. None of this, surely, applies to the novel, which can be read anywhere at all without ritual trappings, and must, if it is any good, eschew the overtly didactic. Yet the experience of reading a novel has certain qualities that remind us of the traditional apprehension of mythology. It can be seen as a form of meditation. Readers have to live with a novel for days or even weeks. It projects them into another world, parallel to but apart from their ordinary lives. They know perfectly well that this fictional realm is not 'real' and yet while they are reading it becomes compelling. A powerful novel becomes part of the backdrop of our lives, long after we have laid the book aside. It is an exercise of make-believe that, like yoga or a religious festival, breaks down barriers of space and time and extends our sympathies, so that we are able to empathise with other lives and sorrows. It teaches compassion, the ability to 'feel with' others. And, like mythology, an important novel is transformative. If we allow it to do so, it can change us forever.

Mythology, we have seen, is an art form. Any powerful work of art invades our being and changes it forever. The British critic George Steiner claims that art, like certain kinds of religious and metaphysical experience, is the most '"ingressive", transformative summons available to human experiencing'. It is an intrusive, invasive indiscretion that 'queries the last privacies of our existence'; an Annunciation that 'breaks into the small house of our cautionary being', so that 'it is no longer habitable in quite the same way as it was before'. It is a transcendent encounter that tells us, in effect: 'change your life'.[108]

If it is written and read with serious attention, a novel, like a myth or any great work of art, can become an initiation that helps us to make a painful rite of passage from one phase of life, one state of mind, to another. A novel, like a myth, teaches us to see the world differently; it shows us how to look into our own hearts and to see our world from a perspective that goes beyond our own self-interest. If professional religious leaders cannot instruct us in mythical lore, our artists and creative writers can perhaps step into this priestly role and bring fresh insight to our lost and damaged world.

References

[1] Mircea Eliade, *The Myth of the Eternal Return or Cosmos and History* (trans. Willard R. Trask, Princeton, 1994), *passim*.

[2] J. Huizinger, *Homo Ludens* (trans. R.F.C. Hall, London), 1949, 5–25.

[3] Huston Smith, *The Illustrated World Religions, A Guide to our Wisdom Traditions* (San Francisco, 1991), 235.

[4] Mircea Eliade, *Myths, Dreams and Mysteries, The Encounter between Contemporary Faiths and Archaic Realities* (trans. Philip Mairet, London, 1960), 59–60.

[5] Ibid., 74.

[6] Mircea Eliade, *Patterns in Comparative Religion* (trans. Rosemary Sheed, London, 1958), 216–19; 267–72.

[7] Ibid., 156–85.

[8] Eliade, *Patterns in Comparative Religion*, 38–58.

9 Rudolf Otto, *The Idea of the Holy, An Inquiry into the non-rational factor in the idea of the divine and its relation to the rational* (trans. John Harvey, Oxford, 1923), 5–41.

10 Eliade, *Myths, Dreams and Mysteries*, 172–8; Wilhelm Schmidt, *The Origin of the Idea of God* (New York, 1912), *passim*.

11 Eliade, *Patterns in Comparative Religion*, 99–108.

12 Eliade, *Myths, Dreams and Mysteries*, 54–86.

13 Joseph Campbell with Bill Moyers, *The Power of Myth* (New York, 1988), 87.

14 Ibid.

15 Eliade, *Myths, Dreams and Mysteries*, 63.

16 Walter Burkert, *Homo Necans, The Anthropology of Ancient Greek Sacrificial Ritual and Myth* (trans. Peter Bing, Los Angeles, Berkeley and London, 1983), 88–93.

17 Ibid., 15–22.

18 Campbell, *The Power of Myth*, 72–74; Burkert, *Homo Necans*, 16–22.

19 Joannes Sloek, *Devotional Language* (trans. Henrik Mossin, Berlin and New York, 1996), 50–52, 68–76, 135.

[20] Walter Burkert, *Structure and History in Greek Mythology and Ritual* (Berkeley, Los Angeles and London, 1980), 90–94; Joseph Campbell, *Historical Atlas of World Mythology; Volume 2: The Way of the Animal Powers; Part 1: Mythologies of the Primitive Hunters and Gatherers* (New York, 1988), 58–80; *The Power of Myth*, 79–81.

[21] Eliade, *Myths, Dreams and Mysteries*, 194–226; Campbell, *The Power of Myth*, 81–85.

[22] Eliade, *Myths, Dreams and Mysteries*, 225.

[23] Campbell, *The Power of Myth*, 124–25.

[24] Burkert, *Homo Necans*, 94–5.

[25] Homer, *The Iliad* 21:470.

[26] Burkert, *Greek Religion*, 149–152.

[27] Burkert, *Homo Necans*, 78–82.

[28] Eliade, *Patterns of Comparative Religion*, 331–343.

[29] Eliade, *Myths, Dreams and Mysteries*, 138–40; *Patterns in Comparative Religion*, 256–261.

[30] Hosea 4:11-19; Ezekiel 8:2-18; 2 Kings 23:4-7.

[31] Eliade, *Myths, Dreams and Mysteries* 161–171; *Patterns in Comparative Religion*, 242–253.

[32] Eliade, *Myths, Dreams and Mysteries*, 162–65.

33 Ibid., 168–171.

34 Ibid., 188–89.

35 Genesis 3:16–19.

36 Anat–Baal Texts 49:11:5; quoted in E.O. James, *The Ancient Gods* (London, 1960), 88.

37 'Inanna's Journey to Hell' in *Poems of Heaven and Hell from Ancient Mesopotamia* (trans. and ed. N.K. Sandars, London, 1971), 165.

38 Ibid., 163.

39 Campbell, *The Power of Myth*, 107–11.

40 Ezekiel 8:14; Jeremiah 32:29, 44:15; Isaiah 17:10.

41 Burkert, *Structure and History*, 109–110.

42 Burkert, *Structure and History*, 123–28; *Homo Necans*, 255–297; *Greek Religion*, 159–161.

43 Eliade, *Myths, Dreams and Mysteries*, 227–8; *Patterns in Comparative Religion*, 331.

44 Karl Jaspers, *The Origin and Goal of History* (trans. Michael Bullock, London, 1953), 47.

45 Gwendolyn Leick, *Mesopotamia, The Invention of the City* (London, 2001), 268.

46 Genesis 4:17.

47 Genesis 4:21–22.

48 Genesis 11:9.

49 Leick, *Mesopotamia*, 22–23.

50 In other epics, Atrahasis is called Ziusudra and Utnapishtim ('he who found life').

51 Thokhild Jacobsen, 'The Cosmos as State' in H. and H.A. Frankfort (eds), *The Intellectual Adventure of Ancient Man, An Essay on Speculative Thought in the Ancient Near East* (Chicago, 1946), 186-197.

52 Ibid., 169.

53 *Enuma Elish*, I:8–11, in Sandars, *Poems of Heaven and Hell*, 73.

54 *Enuma Elish*, VI:19, in Sanders, *Poems of Heaven and Hell*, 99.

55 Isaiah 27:1; Job 3:12, 26:13; Psalms 74:14.

56 Eliade, *Myths, Dreams and Mysteries*, 80–81; *The Myth of the Eternal Return*, 17.

57 *The Epic of Gilgamesh*, I:iv:6, 13, 19, *Myths from Mesopotamia, Creation, the Flood, Gilgamesh, and Others* (trans. Stephanie Dalley, Oxford, 1989), 55.

58 Ibid., I:iv:30–36, p.56.

59 Ibid., VI:ii:1–6, p.78.

[60] Ibid., VI:ii:11–12, p.78-9.

[61] Ibid., XI:vi:4, p.118.

[62] David Damrosch, *The Narrative Covenant. Transformations of Genre in the Growth of Biblical Literature* (San Francisco, 1987), 88–118.

[63] *Epic of Gilgamesh*, XI:ii:6–7 in Dalley, 113.

[64] Ibid., I:9–12, 25–29, p.50.

[65] Ibid., 1:4–7, p.50.

[66] Robert A. Segal, 'Adonis: A Greek Eternal Child' in Dora C. Pozzi and John M. Wickersham (eds), *Myth and the Polis* (Ithaca, New York and London, 1991), 64–86.

[67] Karl Jaspers, *The Origin and Goal of History* (trans. Michael Bullock, London 1953), 1–78.

[68] The author of the *Dao De Jing*, which did not become known until the mid-third century, was using the name of the fictitious sage Laozi, who was often thought to have lived in the late seventh or sixth century, as a pseudonym.

[69] Genesis 18.

[70] Isaiah 6:5; Jeremiah 1:6–10; Ezekiel 2:15.

[71] Confucius, *Analects* 5:6; 16:2.

[72] Sadly, inclusive language is not appropriate

here. Like most of the Axial sages, Confucius
had little time for women.

[73] Confucius, *Analects* 12:22; 17:6.

[74] Ibid., 12:2.

[75] Ibid., 4;15.

[76] Ibid., 8:8.

[77] Ibid., 3:26; 17:12.

[78] *Anguttara Nikaya* 6:63.

[79] *Dao De Jing*, 80.

[80] Ibid., 25.

[81] Ibid., 6, 16, 40, 67.

[82] *Jataka* 1:54–63; *Vinaya: Mahavagga* 1:4.

[83] Psalm 82.

[84] 2 Chronicles 34:5–7.

[85] Hosea 13:2; Jeremiah 10; Psalms 31:6; 115:4–8;
135:15.

[86] Exodus 14.

[87] Isaiah 43:11–12.

[88] Plato, *The Republic*, 10:603D-607A.

[89] Ibid., 522a8; Plato, *Timaeus* 26E5.

[90] *Metaphysics* III, 1000a11–20.

[91] Plato, *The Republic*, 509F.

[92] Plato, *Timaeus* 29B and C.

93 Aristotle, *Metaphysics*, 1074 Bf.

94 2 Corinthians 5:16.

95 Philippians 2:9.

96 Philippians 2:9–11.

97 Philippians 2:7–9.

98 Luke 24:13–22.

99 Kabbalists stressed that En Sof was neither male nor female. It was an 'It' that became a 'Thou' to the mystic at the end of the process of emanation.

100 Gregory of Nyssa, 'Not Three Gods'.

101 Richard S. Westfall, 'The Rise of Science and the Decline of Orthodox Christianity: A Study of Kepler, Descartes and Newton' in David C. Lindberg and Ronald L. Numbers (eds), *God and Nature: Historical Essays on the Encounter Between Christianity and Science* (Berkeley, Los Angeles and London, 1986), 231.

102 Gregory of Nazianzos, *Oration*, 29:6–10

103 Blaise Pascal, *Pensées* (trans. A. J. Krasilsheimer, London, 1966), 209.

104 R.C. Lovelace, 'Puritan Spirituality: The Search for a Rightly Reformed Church' in

Louis Dupre and Don E. Saliers (eds), *Christian Spirituality: Post Reformation and Modern* (London and New York, 1989), 313–15.

[105] T.H. Huxley, *Science and Christian Tradition* (New York, 1896), 125.

[106] Friedrich Nietzsche, *The Gay Science* (New York, 1974), 181.

[107] Thomas Mann, 'The Making of *The Magic Mountain*', in *The Magic Mountain*. (trans. H.I. Lowe Porter, London, 1999), 719-29.

[108] George Steiner, *Real Presences: Is there anything in what we say?* (London, 1989), 142–43.

KAREN ARMSTRONG's first book, the bestselling *Through the Narrow Gate* (1981), described her seven years as a nun in a Roman Catholic order. She has published numerous books, including *A History of God*, which has been translated into thirty languages, *A History of Jerusalem* and *In the Beginning: A New Reading of Genesis*. Her more recent works include *Islam: A Short History* and *Buddha*, which was an international bestseller. Since 1982 she has been a freelance writer and broadcaster. She lives in London.